# JOHN JOYCE

thE LA st gY ppo kiN g

brahma books
los angeles
we bleed ink

4 lOVeRS  SeaRCHeRs bOStoN iRL diASPoRa & THOSE piCKInG LOcKs fORgEd oF stolEn yOUth

The Bait

JOE AND HIS SECOND HUNCH OVER THE PHONE

CUPPED HANDS LIKE THE LAST MATCH LIT IN THE WIND

What is this?

SPORT BARE-KNUCKLE LEAGUE INNA STATES

NOW - LOOK LOOK LOOK LOOK LOOK

Where?

WAIT FER IT

WAIT FER IT
WAIT FER IT

PAUSE IT THERE

jaysus ...

That straw fookin' hat has to
Has to be
Roight then an' there on the fookin' tele
He meant it then?
Had to
Had to have had
Have had to have meant it
Ye don't think?
Aye boyo I t'ink plenty

SILENCE

So it's true then?
What?
He's hangin' around the MMA an' with Conor
Dat's rumors
They say
Dey say fookin' rumors

JOSEPH YER MAN HE'S RIGHT THERE PLAIN AS DAY

LOOKS THE SAME - EXACTLY THE SAME
SAME AS HE WAS ALMOST

What are ye's on about?

SHOULD BE OLDER LOOKIN' THAT'S NOT GOOD

HE SHOULD LOOK FORTY-FIVE
FORTY AT LEAST
LOOKS THIRTY

TOPS

So he's still young an' handsome - ye's in love with him?
Fook sake Joe
What?
I mean he's fit Joe, fit
Aye
Fightin' fit Joe
That's what we want though

A  F I G H T

Is it?
Leave it
Is it Joe?

H E   S T A R E S   A T   T H E   P A U S E D   I M A G E

Is that what we want?

H E   S T A R E S

Maybe that's his kid?
Hunh?
His kid?
There's no kid

N I L

THAT'S HIM
THAT'S HIM

we found him

The Field

THE ACTUAL FOOKIN' ARSE END OF COUNTY WESTMEATH

EVEN SOUNDS IT

M O A T E

BIG JOE AND HIS SECOND SMOKE-TALK-WHISPER AWAY FROM THE BOYS

T H E R E ' S   M E A N T   T O   B E   A   F I G H T

TRAVELLERS
B A R E - K N U C K L E

BETS ARE IN
TALK IS BIG
ONE SIDE'S LATE

Hey Joe! They're not feckin' comin' are ya gonna call it?

N E V E R   Y E   M O I N D   W H A T   I ' M   G O N N A   C A L L

NOW CALM THE BOY DOWN
WE WANT HIM WARMED UP
NOT EXHAUSTED

T H E   B O Y S   N O D   T H E   W O R D S   A Y E   J O E   A Y E   J O E

Ye think he's with Conor n' Kavanaugh?
No maybe dunno but

T H I S   N E W   S P O R T   B A R E - K N U C K L E   L E A G U E

THAT'S OUR LEGACY
THAT'S OUR MONEY

He wouldn't though?
Wouldn't he though?
He might
C'mere to me

C L O S E R

Tell me what ye see
We know at least he's around the fights, Joe
Probably Vegas, we got people in Vegas?
Not him
Boston?
We'd know
New York?
Nil

C A L I F O R N I A ?

Aye Joe California

Los Angeles?
He don't like the heat tho' – maybe San Francisco?
That tan from the video – that's the beach son

H O L L Y W O O D  !

Uh Joe

T H E   B O Y S   E R U P T

D E Y S   A I N ' T   F O O K I N '   C O M I N '

Fook sake
Deys ain't fookin' comin'
Who says?

D E Y S   J U S T   P O S T E D   A   V I D E O

SAYS DIS N' DAT
JUST SHITE DON'T MAKE NO SENSE INNA FIRST PLACE
WE SEEN IT A COUPLE TREE TOIMES NOW
TALKIN' ABOUT NEVER AGREED TO THE LOCATION

T H E Y   W A I T

What ye's feckin' starin' at?
Waitin' fer ya to call it
Foine it's called!

A L L   B E T S   A R E   O F F

SNAP OFF A VIDEO TELLIN' THEY FORFEIT AN' GIVE THE NEEDLE
GIVE IT GOOD
BUT NOT TOO LONG
AN' DON'T YE BE KEEP REPEATIN' YERSELF
CONSTANTLY SAYIN' THE SAME T'ING OVER AN' OVER AGAIN
AN' CONSTANTLY REPEATIN' YERSELF LIKE YE TEND T'DO
LIKE A FECKIN' EEJIT
ONLY A FECKIN' EEJIT REPEATS HISSELF

I N   F A C T   J U N I O R   Y E ' S   D O   T H E   T A L K I N '

THE CIRCUMSTANCE OF THE FORFEITURE

B O Y O

YER YER OWN HYPE MAN
YER TALKIN' SHITE INNA BACKGROUND
GIVE 'EM A LITTLE BOB N' WEAVE
AN' I'M NOT TALKIN' A FOOKIN' HAIRCUT
SHOW 'EM THE MOVES WHAT THEY WANTED NO PART OF

H E   F E E L S   E Y E S   O N   H I M

IS IT STARE AT FECKIN' JOSEPH DAY OR SUMTHIN' ?

Where were we?
Hollywood's not on the beach

FLUMMOXED

Ye coddin' me?

THE SILENT SHAKE OF NO AS BIG JOE SNAPS ONE OFF TO THE BOYS

Oi Junior, on yer bike with the feckin' call-out we're leavin'
What about the money?
I'll be holdin' all the money until a rematch is properly sorted
Yeah but

ANYONE GOT A PROBLEM WITH THAT ?

NO ONE'S GOT A PROBLEM WITH THAT

The Lean

THAT'S IT JOE'S GOT IT - HE HAS IT

he thinks ...

Here's the play we send the kid
To where?
To who
To whom
Fook sake!
To Johnny Boy?

LOS ANGELES

L      O      S      A      N      G      E      L      E      E      E      S

To do what?
To pose, spy - fly on the wall
Spy what?
Johnny Boy's hangin' 'round dat new bare-knuckle league see
Think he's gonna fight?
Maybe, but I t'ink - an' I reckon - an' they been sayin'
Who's they?
Dey who?
They whom
Dey's dose dat's been sayin'
Who's that?
Everyone the feckin' internet who fookin' ever - dat's dey
Well then by all means - what did 'dey' say?
He's there trainin' fookers
Bare-knuckle?
Inna art n' ways o' bare-knuckle - Yanks don't know it like us

HE SAVORS THE WORDS AS HE'S SURE HE'S GOT IT SORTED

SAY HE'S TRAININ' CONOR TOO
GONNA MAKE HIM SWITCH UP AN' JUMP OVER TO THIS NEW LEAGUE SEE
AN' GIVE HIM A PIECE OF THE LEAGUE
THESE YANKS
PERCENTAGE AN' ALL THAT
ENDORSEMENTS WHAT HAVE YE
BRING OVER A BIG STAR

BUT WHAT'S THE MOVE WITH THE KID ?

WE SEND THE KID TO BE TRAINED
SUSS IT OUT
GET THE STORY

HE'LL KNOW

Nil
Aye
This kid is good though - he's gonna do the Boston accent
Why'd he be doin' that?

So's Johnny Boy won't know
He's a Traveller, Joe
Of course he's a Traveller that's why we do the accent
Johnny Boy's from Boston, Joe

BUT HE LIVES IN LOS ANGELES NOW

SO ANOTHER BOSTON BOY
DAT'S THE BOND
THE AFFINITY
HE'LL WANNA BE COACHIN' HIM
PASS THE TORCH AN' ALL

HE'LL BE ABLE TO TELL JOE

THE KID CAN DO IT

    WICKED HAHD
    PAHK THE CAH
    HAHVAHD YAHD

THE WHOLE T'ING
GOOD WILL HUNTIN'

    DONCHA KNOW THEM APPLES?

ALL THAT SHITE — REAL CONVINCIN' TOO

PROPER FOOKIN' CONVINCIN'

I'd have to hear it
Traveller can't play a role? Run a con? Run a scam?
Joe
He can do it
What if he finds out?
Then we'll just lean on him

THE LEAN
WE LEAN ON HIM

What if he runs?

THEN WE'LL KNOW WHERE HE STARTED FROM
AN' WE'LL KNOW WHERE HE LIVES
AN' HE'LL KNOW THAT WE KNOW THAT WE CAN GET TO HIM
THAT WE CAN FIND HIM ANYWHERE

What if he don't care?
What?

WHAT IF HE DON'T CARE ABOUT TRAININ' THE KID?
BARE-KNUCKLE

DON'T GIMME THE LOOK

WHAT IF?

IF  JOE  IF

I'M SAYIN' WHAT IF?
HE WAS JUST AT THE FIGHTS?
LIKE A REGULAR FAN
JUST A GUY WATCHIN' THE FIGHTS?

W H A T   D O   Y E ' S   M E A N   W H A T   I F   H E   D O N ' T   C A R E ?

Joe
He does!
Joe
Even if he don't which he doesn't!
He doesn't don't care?

A   P   O   P   L   E   C   T   I   C

I   F O O K I N '   C A R E

WE'RE FOOKIN' DOIN' THIS
WE'RE DOIN' THIS
WE ARE FOOKIN' DOIN' THIS

H I S   T E E T H   B I T E   H A R D   A L M O S T   K E E P   T H E   W O R D S

i fookin' care ...

T H E   S H A L L O W I N G   O F   H I S   B R E A T H

i am endin' this ...

HIS TALK ALMOST GASP

I   A M   P U T T I N '   T H I S   T '   B E D   F E R   O N C E   A N '   F E R   A L L

What if it's just us thinkin' this?
Bollocks!
What if he doesn't even know?
That we're onto him?
That she died

T H A T   S H E   D I E D

HIS HEAD SHAKES NO
A SERIES OF EVER FASTER SHAKES

NO  NO  NO  NO  NO  NO  NO

W E   A R E   N O T

N E V E R

THE TOIMIN'
THE TOIMIN'
THE TOIMIN'

I T ' S   T H E   T O I M I N '

Could be just a coincidence?

C   O   I   N   C   I   D   E   N   C   E

THERE'S NO SUCH T'ING AS A COINCIDENCE
EVERYTHIN' HAPPENS FER A REASON

E V E R Y T H I N '

HE SEETHES IN THE TIME

it's fate

The Kid

BEAMING WITH PRIDE JOE SHOWS OFF THE KID

I've outdone meself this time if I must say so - an' I must

HIS SHIT-EATING GRIN

Go on say it

HE DOES

THE KID IS FUCKING GOING FOR IT AND IT

GOES LIKE THIS

WICKED HAHD    WICKED TI-YED    WICKED SMAHT

THE SATISFIED GRIN OF THE TONE-DEAF DOING ACCENTS

Joe this is never gonna work
He's great!
Johnny Boy is from Boston, Joe
This kid is sound!

HE'S FROM THERE

EVEN IF HE BOUGHT THE ACCENT
WHICH HE

     NO OFFENSE KID

BUT HE WON'T
BUT EVEN IF HE DID
THE WHOLE LOCAL THING IS GONNA COME UP
OH YEAH?
WHO'S YER DA?
WHAT PART OF THE CITY ARE YE FROM?
DID YE BOX GOLDEN GLOVES?

ALL THE AMERICA SHITE BASEBALL RED SOX WHATEVER

The kid could learn that
Joe he's just an Irish Traveller kid
That's the ticket
What?

IRISH

HE'S AN IRISH KID
HE'S NOT A TRAVELLER

     YER NOT A TRAVELLER
     YER FROM TOWN

HE'S AN ORDINARY IRISH KID GOIN' TO SCHOOL

Have ye met this kid Joe?
Fair play

HE'S GOIN' TO WORK THE TRADES

    GET YE ON THE BUILDIN'S

LOTTA HARDWOOD FLOOR GUYS IS OFF THE BOAT

I N   B O S T O N   J O E   N O T   L O S   A N G E L E S

WE'LL SORT YE SON
YER OVER THE STATES TO MAKE A BUCK IN THE TRADES
AN' YE ALWAYS HEARD ABOUT THE BARE-KNUCKLE AN' YE SEEN HIM
AN' HE'S GONNA TRAIN YE AN' THAT'S HOW YE GET IN
AN' BEFRIEND HIM
YE'S GIVE US THE WORD ON THE WHAT IS WHAT

T H E   L O O K

What now?
He's a bit fat don't ye think?
He is not fat
He's a fat fook Joseph
He's a 'Irish Heavyweight' like me
He don't look like a boxer, Joe
He's not, he's just a regular guy - construction
He's not lookin' like that neither
Jaysus!
He doesn't look like he can run to the toilet if he needs it
We'll start him runnin'

I   S A Y   G E T   A N O T H E R   K I D

THIS ONE

    AGAIN - NO OFFENSE KID

       None taken

THIS KID IS FAT AN' USELESS

       Ya said no offense!

T H E   K I D ' S   A   F A T   U S E L E S S   W A S T E R   I F   E V E R   I   S E E N   O N E

      Hey?

HE'S JUST TOO FECKIN' FAT JOE

      Hey!

This is news to you Fatty McFat-Face with yer wide giant arse?

APPARENTLY IT IS - FATTY IS STUNNED

          I'm standin' roight here!

M A N ' S  A R S E  S H O U L D  N E V E R  B E  W I D E R  T H A N  H I S  S H O U L D E R S

He's supposed to look unsuspectin' not like a gyppo boxer!
Well then mission accomplished he certainly does not

B E T T E R  W E  F I N D  W H E R E  H E  G O E S  F O R  A  D R I N K

GOTTA BE SOME IRISH PLACE
AN' STICK THIS FAT FOOK IN BEHIND THE BAR
ALTHOUGH HE'D LIKELY BE SNEAKIN' OFF TO THE KITCHEN TO NICK CHIPS WITH THAT FAT ARSE OF HIS
STUFFIN' THEM IN HIS FAT FACE

W E  K N O W  P E O P L E  J O E  W E  C A N  S O R T  I T

NO ONE'S BUYIN' THIS FAT FOOK AS AN ATHLETE OR A CONSTRUCTION WORKER

          I'm still roight here!

That's why's I said he's a student!
Joe
Wants to get in shape
Joseph
A college boy he's a bookworm wants to get in shape!

A  S Q U A R E D  P L U S  B  S Q U A R E D  E Q U A L S  ?

C R I C K E T S

AN' HE'S STUPID

          Ya can see me standin' roight here?

I T ' S  C  S Q U A R E D  F A T T Y  A N '  I  D R O P P E D  O U T  F I R S T  Y E A R

HE'S A BAR-BACK OR NOT AT ALL
JOHNNY BOY'S DRUNK HE'LL LOOSEN UP
LESS ON HIS GUARD
THIS KID COMES IN A GYM - JOHNNY BOY WILL SMELL IT AN' BREAK HIS NECK
HE'LL KILL HIM JOE
YE KNOW THAT

H E ' L L  F O O K I N '  K I L L  H I M  D E A D

          Break me neck?

Ye tell me Joe - an' ye tell me now

          Kill me dead?

Aye a bar-back it is

    Hey wait, wait whoa - I don't, uh um

Make it happen

    Joe wait, wait, wait - please?

SHUT YER MOUTH AN' PACK YER BAG FATTY

Yer goin' to America

# The Eighties

THE  SECOND  ENDURES  FATTY  MCFAT-FACE

AN '  HIS  WIDE  GIANT  ARSE

HIS MA WAS FROM TOWN

A M E R I C A N

CITY GIRL
UPTOWN GIRL

        *UPTOWN GIRL*
        *SHE'S BEEN LIVING IN HER UPTOWN WORLD!*

That's a song isn't it?
That's why I sang it
That was singin'?
I wasn't tryna to be good
Then ye feckin' succeeded
Hey!
Suck-ceeded ye done more like it
Sess-seeded is what I done
Ye mean seceded?
Same diff'rence
One's success – one is breakin' away to be yer own country

NOTHING

This a history lesson or what? I asked ya about the eighties!

IF  THERE  WAS  A  FOURTH  WALL  HE'D  BREAK  IT  AND  SAY

THE PROSPECT OF EVEN ATTEMPTIN' TO TRY TO EXPLAIN
THAT THE EIGHTIES WERE AN' ARE – NOW AN' FOREVERMORE – LITERALLY A PART OF HISTORY
TO THIS FAT FOOK IS UNTENABLE
BECAUSE Y'KNOW THAT KID IS THINKIN' KNIGHTS AN' ROMANS WHEN HE SAYS HISTORY
AN' IS PROBABLY PRETTY SURE THEY FOUGHT EACH OTHER

The eighties right, the heyday – the halcyon days
That's pills then isn't it?
What halcyon? No, the proper meanin'
It's pills I told ya
It means a time of great happiness an' contentment
That explain the drug takin' it fer a name – it's sleepin' pills

*don't say it he's not gonna get it ...*

IT ACTUALLY MEANS A PARTICULAR FOURTEEN-DAY PERIOD
AROUND THE WINTER SOLSTICE
WHEN THE KINGFISHER BUILDS ITS NEST
AN' THE OCEAN WATERS ARE CALM

Wait that's a bird then?
Yes the kingfisher's a bird

It catches fish then?
Aye
How's he do it?

J A Y S U S   M A R Y   N '   J O S E P H

IT FLIES UP REALLY HIGH
COMES DOWN REALLY FAST
DIVES DOWN INTO THE WATER
GRABS A FISH COMES UP

How does it know where the fish are?

*this fat fook will be the death of me ...*

How does it know?
Magic
What?

ANCIENT CELTIC FAIRY BIRD MAGIC
IT KNOWS
IT'S A MAGIC BIRD
WITH MAGICAL MYSTICAL POWERS

That's why it's the king?
Indeed son, indeed - well done
Even better name for the drug since it's also y'know magical
Aye son those marketin' fellas really sorted it

*why in the fook did i say halcyon days?*

*should have just said the eighties were the shite ...*

So the eighties was the shite then?
Aye ye've no idea
If ya's sendin' me over ya better give me the back story
Disagree, what if ye say somethin' yer not supposed to know?
Why would I do that?
Yer a bit daft
Hey?
Not exactly university material
I mean that's what they say but
But nothin' this is Joe's thing - his idea sendin' ye over
But Johnny Boy's from over there half Traveller from his ma right?
No she was from town

U P T O W N   G I R L ?

Oh right ya said that when I was singin'

H I S   D A   W A S   A   T R A V E L L E R

TRAVELLER AS IT GETS
AN' THEN SOME

HE WENT OVER TO THE STATES
SCAMS AN' RACKETS
SMALL LUCRATIVE ALWAYS ON THE MAKE

SEE THE EIGHTIES WERE A BIG DRUG TIME

HE GOT IN OVER THERE WITH THE POT THING
DOIN' VERY WELL
HOUSE BY THE BEACH
THE PORSCHE

The Panamera?
No they didn't make that yet the other one
The 911?
That's it the 911 Targa
The Targa that's the shite – what's a Targa?
It's the removable roof
A convertible!
Nay it's not a convertible
Ya said the roof goes down
It doesn't go down it comes off
Why don't they fold it down?
The top piece pops off ye put it in the boot
That's a convertible
It doesn't fold down it's not the whole roof just the middle
But it converts?

HE HAD THE FECKIN' TARGA !

SILENCE

ANYWAYS HE GOT PINCHED
OR RATHER SOME IN HIS CREW GOT PINCHED
THEY TURNED STATES ON HIM

They seceded turned their states into a country?

JAYSUS KID

Sorry

THEY GAVE HIM UP
THEY RATTED HIM OUT
SO THEY COULD GET OFF

He went in then?
Aye

AN' HE KEPT HIS MOUTH SHUT

A GOOD MAN
A PROPER MAN

A PROPER MAN

HE WASN'T SURE ABOUT ALL THE DRUG DEALERS THAT HE WAS ALIGNED WITH
BEIN' THAT SOMEONE RATTED HIM
DONE THE DIRT ON HIM
SO HE SENT THE WIFE AN' KID

Johnny Boy right?
It's not a quiz
Right sorry

HE SENT 'EM OVER WITH SOME MONEY AN' A LETTER
HE'D ALWAYS SEND MONEY HOME
WE TOOK 'EM IN
AN' SEE WE MOVED MORE BACK THEN
THEN IT WAS STILL CARAVANS AN' WAGONS EVEN
THERE'S NO WAY SOME MIAMI DRUG GUY IS GONNA FIND 'EM
NOR SOME BOSTON FBI MAN
WE CAN JUST DISAPPEAR
NO SET LOCATION
NO PAPER TRAIL

A C T I V I S T S   S E E   -   E S P E C I A L L Y   T H E N

SEE US
SEE TRAVELLERS
SEE THEM ACTIVISTS SAYS
WE TRAVELLIN' PEOPLES ARE MARGINALIZED
DISENFRANCHISED

Like McDonalds?
What?
Franchised?

U N - F E C K I N ' - B E L I E V E A B L E

FOOK SAKE
IF YE HAD ONE BIT A' SENSE IN THAT BRAIN OF YERS
IT WOULD DIE OF FECKIN' LONELINESS

L E G A L L Y

AN' LOTSA WAYS
TRAVELLIN' PEOPLE OFTEN DON'T EXIST
IN THE SYSTEM FOR SERVICES
HEALTH
TAX
EMPLOYMENT
SCHOOLS
VACCINES
THE WORLD OF TOWN

A   W O R L D   I N   W H I C H   W E   D O   N O T   B E L O N G

THESE DO-GOODERS ARE TRYIN' TO GET US TO BELONG TO SOMETHIN' WE WANT NO PART OF

TO SETTLE US AGAINST OUR WISHES

THEY PASSED AN ACT - SOME LAWS IN 1980 TO SETTLE US

IT WAS ACTUALLY CALLED THE FINAL SOLUTION

PRINTED RIGHT THERE IN THE TITLE OF THE LEGISLATION
WELL WE HEARD THAT ONE BEFORE

THE FINAL SOLUTION

LIKE THEY DONE WITH THE JEWS

like they done to us in europe - nobody even knows that

HAD IT RIGHT THERE ON THE ACTUAL DOCUMENTS - THE LEGAL PAPERWORK
NOT EVEN TRYIN' TO HIDE IT

WE ARE A PEOPLE

THERE'S TRAVELLERS
REAL ROMANI
IN HUNGARY
THAT STILL DOES THE WAGONS WITH THE HORSES
PROPER TINKER WAGONS
THE VANNERS AN' THE VARDOS
THE OLD WAYS
BEEN DOIN' IT FOR THOUSANDS OF YEARS
WE ARE A NATION WITH NO BORDERS
A NATION WITH NO LAND
BUT THEM ACTIVISTS SAYS IT'S BAD

THEM ACTIVISTS SAYS IT'S WRONG

But they don't see the value?
Aye now yer suckin' diesel

*he was so happy he got it he forgot what the fook he was talkin' about*

Wait so what is the value?

YER OFF THE MAP

YER NOT IN THEIR GAME
YE DON'T EXIST
AN' IF YER IN A JAM
WITH THE DEA
FBI
AN' SOME DRUG ASSOCIATES
CIRCA NINETEEN EIGHTY-NINE
AN' YE NEED TO DISAPPEAR

INTO THE IRISH MIST

L E A V I N '   N O   T R A C E

WE'VE GOT CONNECTIONS TO TRIBES DEEP IN THE INLAND COUNTIES
EUROPE
CZECH REPUBLIC
ROMANIA
TRANSYLVANIA

Like Dracula?
I swear to god son I am goin' to slap ye
Sorry

WE ARE A NATION

W E   A R E   A   P E O P L E   N O   M A T T E R   W H A T   T H E Y   S A Y

A NA LUCHT SIÚIL
THE WALKIN' PEOPLE IN GAELIC
PAVEE
MINCIÉRS
THE MINCÉIRI - IN THE SHELTA CANT
WE'VE OUR OWN LANGUAGE
THE GAMMON

M Y D I L   M I N C É I R I   T A S H L E R

SAY IT SON    SAY IT    SAY IT WITH ME

I ' M   A   P R O U D   I R I S H   T R A V E L L E R

YE NEED TO KEEP UP WITH THE GAMMON BOYO
WHATEVER ISSUES WE MAY HAVE WITH EACH OTHER
WE'RE UNITED AGAINST THE OUTSIDE

W E   T A K E   C A R E   O F   O U R   O W N

So they came over? Johnny Boy an' his ma?

A Y E

SHE HATED IT
BUT ADAPTED WELL

Joe didn't like her bein' not a Traveller?

SON A TRAVELLER JUST DOESN'T

D O E S   N O T

MARRY SOMEONE FROM TOWN

A N   A M E R I C A N   A T   T H A T   I T   J U S T   D O E S N ' T   H A P P E N

JOE HATED BIG JOHN 'CUZ OF IT

BUT HE LOVED THOSE ENVELOPES
EVERY MONTH
LIKE CLOCKWORK
HE SOMETIMES TALKED OF IT LIKE A TRIBUTE
IT WASN'T
JOE'S GOT A WEAKNESS FOR PRETTY GIRLS

AN'  SHE  WAS  BEUATIFUL  FOR  A  START

SO HE HATED HER FOR THAT AS WELL
SHE HATED HIM RIGHT BACK
SHE HAD HIS NUMBER
AN' HE HATED HER FOR BEIN' SMART ENOUGH TO HAVE IT

She was smart?

SMARTER  THAN  BIG  JOHN  WHO  WAS  SHARP  AS  A  BLADE

QUICK CAGEY DANGEROUS
HE COULD FIGHT YE
YE COULDN'T MUSCLE HIM
HE'S ALSO SMART TOO
NOT LIKE HIS WIFE BUT ENOUGH
SO HE HAD IT ON THE STREET LEVEL
THE HUSTLE THE FIGHTIN'
HAD THE BODY
THE GUTS
AN' HE HAD THE CHARM TOO
HE HAD THE VERBALS
BOYO HE COULD TALK
TALK YE INTO ANYTHIN'

He talked ya into takin' them in?

DIDN'T  HAVE  TO  HE  WAS  GYPSY  KING  -  TOP  FIGHTER

What about Joe?
Joe got it when he left - they never actually fought
Who would have won?
Tough to say, maybe Joe
That's a no
Yer not so stupid after all
Johnny Boy's da would have killed him
Plus he'd send money back like ye said? He did the right thing?

ALWAYS  DID  RIGHT  BY  THE  CLAN

THE BLOOD
YE KNOW
THE BLOOD
THE BLOOD

YE  DON'T  EVER  TURN  YER  BACK  ON  THE  BLOOD

Then why are we tryin' to set up Johnny Boy?



Ah shite me phone!
Ya phone didn't ring!
It's on vibrate
Ya said ya was gonna tell me about the eighties!
We'll meet again - I'll tell ye some other time
If we's a tribe an' a nation why ya doin' the dirt on Johnny Boy?
Stop actin' the maggot
What about the eighties?
Fook off I'm busy
Ya guys are feckin' secedin' Johnny Boy
On yer bike fatty - fook' off I said
Ya said ya tell me about the eighties!

HATE  TO  BREAK  IT  TO  YE  FATTY

BUT IT ALL WENT DOWN IN

N I N E T E E N   E I G H T Y  -  N I N E

The eighties was feckin' over

N l n 9 T e E n

e I 8 h T y - 9 I n E

# The Fair

W H E N   T H E Y   A R R I V E D   I T   W A S   J U S T   S U M M E R

EARLY JUNE THE GYPSIES HAD THEIR FAIR IN THE UK
JOE'S TRIBE STAYED BEHIND INLAND COUNTY GALWAY NEAR ROSCOMMON
IT RUBBED PEOPLE WRONG 'CUZ APPLEBY IS BIG

B I G   J O H N ' S   W I F E   N '   K I D   C O M I N '   O V E R   W A S   B I G

SO'S THE MONEY HE PAID JOE

T H E   ' L O O K I N '   A F T E R '   M O N E Y

AN' HE ALWAYS PAID THE MONTHLY - BEFORE HE WENT IN
THEY'D ALL BE BACK THIS WAY IN THE FALL FOR BALLINASLOE
HE'D BUY ANY HORSE HE FANCIED THEN - EVEN THO' HE SPENT THE WAD ON FOUR NEW CARAVANS

F O R   H I M S E L F   -   F O R   H I M   A N '   H I S

SUPPOSED TO BE FOR BIG JOHN'S WIFE AN' KID
BUT WHAT DID THEY KNOW FROM A CARAVAN?
THEY COULD HAVE HIS OLD ONE

T H E Y ' D   H A V E   T H E I R   O W N   S U M M E R   F A I R

I T   E X C I T E D   T H E   C L A N   -   W H I C H   E X C I T E D   J O E

FLASHIN' RACES HORSE DEALS
GAMES FIGHTS FORTUNE TELLERS
THE MUSIC THE DANCIN'
GOOD CRAIC
THEY'D HAVE THE LOT

W O R D   G O T   S E N T   ' R O U N D   A N '   T H E   O T H E R   C L A N S   C A M E

HE PROMISED CHARMED HUSTLED
PULLED FAVORS
ABSOLVED DEBTS
LEANED ON OTHERS
CALLED IN HIS CHIPS

T H E   C L A N S   W O U L D   S E E   T H E   A M E R I C A N S

THE TRAVELLERS WOULD SHOW THE YANKS

H E ' D   S H O W   T H E M

THEY'D SEE THE SIZE OF HIS CLAN

H I S   P O W E R   T O   G E T   S O   M A N Y   T R I B E S   T O   N O T   G O   T O   A P P L E B Y

HIS TOP LINE CARAVANS
HIS HORSES
HIS SONS

THE  SKY  DRESSED  FALL  IN  JUNE

ON A CLOUDY DAY THE MISTY SKY CAN SHINE
THERE'S WATER IN THE AIR

REFLECTS  REFRACTS

THE SHINE OF HER PALE SKIN CAUGHT HIM
FLASHING EYES AND SMILE

        *MY LOVE SAID TO ME*
        *MY MOTHER WON'T MIND*

Let's get a look at the Yank!
They say his da's a gangster
Yer da's a tinker
Yers is a horse stealer - I mean dealer

THE  GIGGLE  LIGHT  LAUGHTER  OF  TEENAGE  GIRLS

        *AND ME FATHER WON'T SLIGHT YOU*
        *FOR YOUR LACK OF KIND*

Wish I was dressed then
I don't t'ink he minds Lo'
Says the girl in her gypsy skirt, lashes n' makeup up ya sexy girl
I'm all muck boots an' jumpers
So's everyone
Me hair's a state - he'll t'ink I'm just dust n' donkeys
I dare ya t' kiss him
No!
Double dare!

p i N K y  s W e a R !

UNLOCKED  FINGERS  FREE  HER  SHE  TURNS  TO  HIM

*god she's coming ...*

ALL  BLUSH  CHEEKS  AND  TEETH

Hey Boston howiye?

SHESMILELAUGHGIGGLESQUEALCLOSEDEYEWHISPERSHIM

It's fer a bet

SHE  KISSES  HIS  NECK

*yer deadly ...*

        *THEN SHE STEPPED AWAY FROM ME*
        *AND THIS SHE DID SAY*

SHE FLUTTER - FLOATS BACK TO HER FRIEND

Go away ya didn't!
Bet's a bet
Yer blushin'
Am I?

SCARLET GIRL SCARLET

Wasn't the lips
Kiss is a kiss
What'd ya whisper?
That he's deadly
Ya think he'd fancy me?
Too late - I licked him he's mine
Claimed him then?
Is he lookin'?

BLUSHING

He's a happy boy
Bring him 'round the harness races for ya?
I can't too distractin'
Give him the craic - get the story all the particulars
Ya trust me alone with the deadly American?
He's bleedin' deadly

THE SQUEAL AND JOY OF SIXTEEN SEVENTEEN

PLEASE THE CRAIC
I'M OFF
MEET ME LATER
GO
GO GET HIM
BYE BYE BYE

    *IT WILL NOT BE LONG LOVE*
    *TILL OUR WEDDING DAY*

*she is so beautiful*

    *SHE STEPPED AWAY FROM ME*
    *AND SHE MOVED THROUGH THE FAIR*

Howiye?
What's her name?
Loa

HE WHISPERED IT OVER AND OVER IN HIS MIND

*loa*

LIKE A TREASURED SECRET LIKE A SECRET TREASURE

THE SOUND OF HER NAME
ITS BEAUTY

GOT HIM LOST

Huh?
I said she fancies ya
Loa?

HE LIKED HOW HE FELT WHEN HE SAID IT

THE BLACK MARIA'S WHAT THEY CALL ME
I SEEN YER MA
SHE'S CLASS
YER DA'S A LEGEND 'ROUND HERE

Hey where's she going?

HORSES

CART RACES
HARNESS RACIN'
FLASHIN' TRADIN' DEALIN' STEALIN'
HER FAM'S ALL ABOUT THE HORSES

SHE GRABS HIS ARM

Come with me show ya 'round
Can we go see her racing?
She says yer too distractin'

LET'S GO THEY'RE SIZIN' YA UP

Who?

EVERYONE

Y'ever been the new kid?
Yeah
Had to fight?
Yeah
Can ya fight?
My dad's a legend
Ya say dad not da - I love it!
Yeah?
So what's the story America?
What story?
What's goin' on over there - what's big?
MTV
Em we got television here too y'know - it's not the dark ages

QUICKLY NOW LET'S KEEP MOVIN'

You look like a gypsy fortune teller
I am a gypsy fortune teller!
What was the bet?
I bet her to kiss ya
What'd she win?
Braggin' rights – the satisfaction of a job well done

H O W E V E R

IT WASN'T A PROPER KISS
WASN'T THE LIPS

H E R   T E E T H   S C R A P E   S O F T   O N   H E R   B O T T O M   L I P

c'mere to me

K I S S   M E

T H E Y   K I S S E D   L O N G E R   A N D   H O T T E R   T H A N   T H E Y   S H O U L D

ESPECIALLY FOR A BOY WHO JUST FELL MADLY IN LOVE WITH SOMEONE ELSE

H E R   B O D Y   L I T   U P   A S   S H E   B R O K E   O F F   F O R   A I R

JAYSUS
THAT'S CLASS
THAT'S GRAND
COME
YA DONE FINE
YA PASSED THE TEST BOYO

THE SLIGHTEST CHANGE IN HER AS SHE LETS GO OF THE MOMENT SHE SAYS WITHOUT LOOKING AT HIM

L I S T E N   T H E Y ' R E   W A T C H I N '

NONE TOO PLEASED AT ALL THE ATTENTION YER GETTIN'
BUT THEY'S GONNA FIGHT YA ANYWAY
TEST YA
INITIATION

Who?
The Boys
Who's the boys?
Joe's Boys
Big Joe?
Tá
His sons?
Aye his crop o' bastards the Joe Juniors
The Joe Juniors?

T H E R E ' S   F E C K I N '   T W O   O F   ' E M

TWO SONS FROM TWO DIFF'RENT MUDDERS
AN' THEY BOTH WANTED TO CLAIM THE NAME

IT'S VERY VERY TRAVELLER
THEY WALK AROUND LIKE PRINCES
THEY'RE HIS MUSCLE
THEY'RE BOTH GONNA FIGHT YA
'TIS BUT A SMALL PRICE TO PAY

FER TWO BEAUTIFUL TRAVELLER GIRLS SHIFTIN' YA

RIGHT HERE COME'S

MIKEY THE PIKEY BIKEY
he's gonna introduce himself exactly that way ...

WELCOME WELCOME JOHNNY BOY WELCOME

MIKEY THE PIKEY BIKEY'S THE NAME !

Told ya
Cool motorcycle

THEY CACKLE LAUGH

m o T O r C y c L e !

THAT'S YANK - CALLS A MOTORBIKE A MOTORCYCLE
BIG FAN O' YER DA
Y'EVER NEED ANYTHIN' BIKE RELATED

A PROPER MOTORBIKE ?

I SPECIALISE IN QUALITY - SHALL WE SAY ...

PRE - OWNED INVENTORY

YOU COULD HEAR THE WINK AND THE GLEE

He adores nickin' motorbikes
I truly do it is me gift

ANYTHIN' JOHNNY BOY

BOOTS LEATHERS PARTS ANYTHIN'
GET THEM FROM ME
BUY SELL TRADE
LIKE BASICALLY Y'SEE IT'S LIKE THESE ARE ME HORSES
THE WAY THE OTHERS ARE Y'KNOW WITH THE VANNERS AN' ALL
LOOK BOYO I'M ON YER SIDE

THEY'S COMIN' FER YE SON

When?
Now
Right now?

MIKEY'S   KNOWING   NOD

THEY'S WALKIN' OVER SON

IT'S   BIG   IT'S   MAD

THEY EVEN PAUSED THE REST OF THE RACIN' 'TIL AFTER

THEY   ARE   GONNA   CHALLENGE   YE

IT'LL BE FAIR THO'

MOSTLY

LIKE A BIT O' SPARRIN'
YE DON'T HAVE TO WIN
YE JUST HAVE TO SHOW CLASS
HANG IN TRY NOT T'BE TERRIBLE

HE   COMES   CLOSE   TO   WHISPER

the first joe junior will be the spar - watch fer dat thumb in yer eye ...

THE   CLAN   BEGINS   TO   CIRCLE

IF YE WIN OR EVEN SURVIVE IT
YE WON'T
NO SHAME IN THAT
BUT IF YE MAKE IT THROUGH
THE OTHER JOE JR WILL BE THE REAL FOIGHT
PROPER FOIGHT
PROPER BARE-KNUCKLE SEE
BUT YE'LL BE TIRED AN' CUT UP FROM THE

FRIENDLY   SPAR

IT'LL BE OVER QUICK
THEN YE'LL BE IN
ONE OF US
AS MUCH AS YE CAN

          *AND FONDLY I WATCHED HER*
          *MOVE HERE AND MOVE THERE*

LOA   BACK   FROM   THE   CANCELLED   RACES

FLOATING
IN THE BLACK MARIA'S HASTILY BORROWED CLOTHES
BLUSHING SMILING

ECSTATIC   LOA

LOCKS HER ARMS TO THE BLACK MARIA'S
THE SIGHT OF THEM

A SIGHT TO SEE
EVERYONE CIRCLED TO WATCH
TO WATCH THEM WATCH HIM

TO   WATCH   HER   WATCH   HIM

          *AND SHE WENT HER WAY HOMEWARD*
          *WITH ONE STAR AWAKE*

I got the shift
Go away!
Had to - score
Deadly?
Lethal

H E Y   B O S T O N   W H A T ' S   T H E   S T O R Y ?

SHE TIES HER SCARF AROUND HIS NECK

U N B U T T O N S   H I S   C H A M B R A Y   S H I R T   A   N O T C H   O R   T W O

NOW YER NEARLY ALMOST READY

they'll both cheat ...

YOU'LL SEE IT COMIN' FROM THE BIG ONE
HE'S NOT AT ALL CLEVER BUT HE'S DANGEROUS

the little one's devious ...

S H E   K I S S E S   H I S   L I P S

she whispers him luck - kusthi bok - now yer ready

I F   T H E R E   W A S   A   G A E L I C   O R   T R A V E L L E R   W O R D   F O R   M O O K

IT'D BE - THE JOE JUNIORS - PLURAL

A N D   J U S T   L I K E   T H A T   I T   W A S   O N

*stare his eyes - pin him down*
*move move*
*stay loose*
*they're betting?*
*the fuck is he barking?*
*ignore it*
*ignore them*
*ignore it all*

B I G   J O E   W A T C H E S

MIKEY THE PIKEY BIKEY WAS TELLIN' HIM THE RULES
THE TERMS
THE THIS AND THAT

JOHNNY  BOY  JUST  KINDA  NODDED  ALONG

SOMEONE   SAID   FIGHT   AND   IT   WENT

JOHNNY BOY THOUGHT THE WHOLE THING WAS A SCAM
AN' WASN'T GONNA HIT ANYONE WITHOUT BEIN' HIT FIRST
FIGURED THE WHOLE TRIBE WAS GONNA JUMP HIM
EXCEPT LITTLE JOE JR COULDN'T HIT HIM
COULD NOT GET NEAR HIM
LOOKED SICK NEXT TO THE YANK
EMACIATED
JOHNNY BOY WAS FIT

LOOK  AT  HIM  MOVE  HE  FLOATS

HUFF HUFF
SWING

*he's lunging ...*

SWING

*he's slow ...*

JAB JAB

*pull it back miss on purpose - don't hit until he hits you*

TOIME!

Ye's need to foight son – it's not shadow boxin'!
You said friendly

WE  SAID  A  FRIENDLY  FOIGHT  SON

FRIENDLY
AYE
BUT AN ACTUAL FOIGHT

READY ?

NODS

FOIGHT!

MOVE  MOVE  SWING  SWING  MISS  MISS

*make him chase*
*make him miss*
*he's hyper*
*outta breath*
*leaning lunging missing*
*keeps spitting on the ground*

*oh he's fucking wasted ...*

PAD  PAD  FEET  FEET

F I G H T I N G ' S   M O R E   F E E T   T H A N   H A N D S

CIRCLE  CIRCLE

*fuck it you want a fight?*

P A P   P A P

T H E   E Y E

OOHHH!  OOHHH!

T H E   C R O W D   E R U P T S

*finish it - there's another one waiting trying to see the moves*

P A P

T H E   N O S E

OOHHHHHHHH!

*he's hurt*
*in bare-knuckle you have to pick your shots - every punch could break your hand*
*fake the left*

E L B O W S   U P   T O   B L O C K   T H E   H O O K

*right hand straight down the middle*

P A P

S P L I T   T H E   L I P S   B O T H   H A N D S   B L O O D

BENDS FORWARD

*left to the gut*

LIVER SHOT DROPS HIM

I T ' S   O V E R

THE CROWD TOO SHOCKED TO SOUND IT

G E T   U P   G E T   U P   G E T   U P

THE CROWD RUSHES HIM

L A U G H I N G   C O A C H I N G   S C R E A M I N G

T O I M E !

TOIME TOIME TOIME TOIME

T O I M E   I   S A Y S

T O I M E !

GET UP SON
YER A TRAVELLER
GET UP GET UP
HE'S A YANK
YE FECKIN' EMBARRASSMENT
FOIGHT HIM SON FOIGHT HIM
STAND UP

W E   S A I D   F R I E N D L Y   W E   S A I D   F R I E N D L Y

HE DONE THE DIRT ON HIM
HE DONE THE DIRT ON HIM

A   T U M U L T   O F   B U L L S H I T

THEY HUDDLE COMPARING THE QUICKEST LIES AND EXCUSES

B I G   J O E

WAVES BOTH HANDS
WAVES IT OFF

N O   C O N T E S T

JOHNNY BOY'S FOCUS FADES THE DIN
HE COULD ALWAYS DO THIS
CHAOS FADES TO SOFT STATIC
AND HE JUST STARES THE NEXT MOTHERFUCKER DOWN

H E   B E A S T S   H I S   W A Y   T H R O U G H   T H E   C R O W D

*fuck that's a big dude ...*

*holy shit*
*fuck him*
*stay in it*
*eyes on eyes*
*don't blink*
*don't break*

J O E   H I S   S E C O N D   A N D   M I K E Y   H U D D L E

*someone's talking*
*they're always talking*
*they never shut up*

*i feel loa and the black maria ...*

*don't look*
*stay in it*
*stay in it*
*times slows when you're this in it*
*stay in this time*

*i love when time is like this ...*

*stay in it*

*eyes on eyes*
*he's scared*
*confused*

*i got him ...*

*he already lost*
*he'll cheat she said*
*but no one thought i'd win*

*except me*

*stay eyes*
*stay here*
*don't blink*
*don't even think about*

C H I N   F L I P   C H I N   F L I P

YEAH? YEAH?
YOU NEXT? YOU NEXT?

Y O U ' L L   N E V E R   H I T   M E   A S   H A R D   A S   M Y   D A D

E V E R Y   T I N K E R   H E A R D   T H A T

EVERY SINGLE FOOKIN' ONE
IT WOKE 'EM UP
THEY ALL JUST REMEMBERED THAT THIS WHIP-THIN WIRY

K I D

MOVES LIKE THE WIND
AIN'T NO YANK LIKE OUR EGOS TOLD US
AIN'T NO PRETTY BOY LIKE OUR EYES SHOWED US

T H I S   W A S   B I G   J O H N ' S   S O N

HE WAS TAUGHT TO FIGHT THE HARD WAY
BY A PROPER MAN

T H I S   B O Y   W A S   H A R D   A S   F U C K

IT ALL COMES FROM SOMEWHERE
YE DON'T LICK IT OFF THE ROCKS
LIKE I SAID EVERY TINKER HEARD THAT
KNEW WHAT IT MEANT

I N C L U D I N '   T H I S   O N E

AN' INCLUDIN' THE ONE IN FRONT OF HIM

*he blinked ...*

*he broke ...*

*i win*

JOHNNY BOY PUT HIS HAND UP

F I S T   T O   T H E   S K Y   -   J U S T   S T A R E D   A T   H I M

*he's talking to someone*
*joe and his guy*
*joe's guy*
*his second*
*has to be the brains*
*stay in it*
*find his eyes*
*laser beam him through his dad*
*burn him down*
*stay in it*

J O E ' S   V O I C E   S I M M E R E D   I N   T H E   B A C K R O U N D   A   M U R M U R

NOW NOW JOE JR IS A CHAMPION
AN' HE'S NOT GONNA JUST FOIGHT FER NOTHIN'
AN' THIS JOHNNY BOY
HE DIDN'T KNOW ABOUT A FRIENDLY
SO NOW THIS HERE'S PERSONAL
AS GOIN' SO HARD CONSTITUTES CHEETIN' BY THE YANK
AN' NOW WE'S IN A PROPER FOIGHT
SO THERE NEEDS TO BE SOME STAKES

*that mikey guy's near me ...*

THEY'RE SCRAMBLIN' TO SAVE FACE
SAYIN' THAT YE WENT HARD ON A 'FRIENDLY'
THAT YE DONE THE DIRT ON HIM
BUT THEIR WHOLE PLAN WAS THEY WAS GONNA DO THE DIRT ON YE INNA FIRST PLACE
AN' NOW THEY'S HOPIN' - BEIN' A KID
YE WON'T HAVE A BIG ENOUGH BET ON YE TO 'BUY IN'
THEN OTHER JOE JR AIN'T GOTTA FOIGHT YE
AT LEAST NOT TODAY

T H E Y ' S   L O O K I N '   F E R   A N   O U T   S O N

WANT ME T'DO YER TALKIN' FER YE?
BE YER SECOND?

HE   NODS   HIM   A   YEAH   YEAH   SURE   WHATEVER

SOUND FADES BACK INTO THE SLOW MOTION TIME AS JOE BEGINS TO SPEAK

*he'll look*
*he'll look*
*there you are*
*how's my eyes motherfucker?*
*i fucking dare you to stare me down*

JOE   TRIES   TO   SELL   IT

AN' AS SEEIN' ON ACCOUNT THE YOUNG MAN DOESN'T HAVE THE MONEY
AN' DIDN'T UNNERSTAN' PROPERLY
WE'RE GOIN' TO CALL IT

ONE   HUNDRED   PUNTS !

LOA

SHE   WON   IT   AT   THE   RACES

Now now this is not the type a sitch-eee-ation
I've one hundred punts on Boston!

THE   CROWD   SNAPS   ALIVE   ELECTRIC

Any takers?

TIME AROUND THE CROWD NOW SLOWS TO THE TIME THAT JOHNNY BOY STAYS IN

THEY   WANT   IT

THE ACTION
THE FIGHT
THE BETS
THEY WANNA SEE JOHNNY BOY FIGHT AGAIN

THEY   WANNA   SEE   IF   OTHER   JOE   JR   PUSSIES   OUT

I'VE ANOTHER FIFTAY ON JOHNNY BOY!

THE   BLACK   MARIA

THE HUSTLE EXPLODES THE CROWD INTO WAVES
THE ACTION
THE TAKERS
THE SIDE BETS
CASH FROM POCKETS AND PURSES MONEY IN THE HAND
MONEY WAVING THERE
MONEY LIGHTS A FIRE IN THE CROWD

NOW THERE'S SO MUCH MONEY YOU CAN'T WALK AWAY

CAN'T TALK YOUR WAY OUT OF IT

MIKEY'S BACK

HE LEANS IN FOR THE WHISPER - JOHNNY BOY WHISPERS IT QUICK

THE NOD AND GRIN OF A SCAMMER

I SAY THAT'S A GRAND IDEA SON
NOT QUITE THE SAME THRILL AS LIBERATIN' A BIKE FROM THE PAVEMENT
BUT STILL PRETTY FOOKIN' GRAND

PUN INTENDED
*what pun ye might say?*

MIKEY SAYS

JOHNNY BOY'S GOT

ONE THOUSAND AMERICAN

ON HIMSELF - AIN'T IT GRAND?

BEFORE ANYONE CAN EVEN THINK TO BEGIN TO REACT

TO QUESTION IT
TO ASK
TO SEE IT
TO COUNT WHAT THAT MEANS IN PUNTS

JOHNNY BOY LITERALLY WALKS RIGHT UP

THROWS IT AT HIM

TEN PERFECTLY CRISP

AMERICAN ONE-HUNDRED DOLLAR BILLS

PRETTIEST GREEN THERE IS NOT EVEN IRELAND HERSELF'S AS PRETTY GREEN AS THAT AMERICAN MONEY

You got a thousand?
There'll be a rematch
Fuck you old man this is it

SPITS AT JOE JR WHILE HE SHOOTS THE LOOK AT JOE

THIS IS YOUR SHOT
THIS IS IT
NOW THROW DOWN A THOUSAND OR GET THE FUCK OUT OF MY FACE

THEY'RE ARGUING HE'S DONE NEITHER ONE WANTS IT

JOE GRABS HIS SON'S LEATHER
GRABS HIS HEAD BY THE BACK OF THE NECK
TRIES TO HISS THE FIGHT INTO HIS SON
OTHER JOE JUNIOR PIVOTS PULLS AND PIVOTS AGAIN
HE RIPPED HIS JACKET FROM BIG JOE'S MASSIVE HAND
HUNG HIS HEAD AND WALKED AWAY


BOOS JEERS MOCKING HIM SLAPPED WITH FANNED MONEY

CHANTS OF

    jOHNnY  BoY
    JoHnNy  bOy
    jOhnNy  Boy
    JoHNny  bOy

PEOPLE THREW SHIT
TOSSED DRINKS IN JOE JR'S FACE
SPIT AT HIM
MOCKED HIM
CURSED HIM OUT IN THE SHELTA CANT - THE GAMMON
SOMEONE MADE A SHOW OF IT AND PULLED A 'JOHHNY BOY'

TOSSING  ONE  PUNT  NOTES  AT  HIS  MASSIVE  BACK

OTHERS RUSHED TO JOHNNY BOY PICKING HIM UP CHANTING AGAIN

T   I   M   E

A  BLUR  OF  DRINKS  AND  STORIES  LATER

THE CRAIC
THE LASH

THEN  CALMER  'ROUND  THE  FIRE

DiD ya SEE tHAT?
He NEVER No NeVer hE BeAt him
hE rAN AwAy He wON fOOk alL
HE DidN'T dO fOOk aLL tHE FiRSt JoE jR wAS supPoSEd tO BE A FriENdLy
tHEy're TaLKin' sHite tHat's A WiN
HE WOn FOOk All
yE cAN't LOSe A FoigHT ThAt dIDn'T hAPPeN!

AROUND  ANOTHER  DIFFERENT  YOUNGER  FIRE

What's Boston words?
Wicked this wicked that
Like what?
Wicked cool or wicked awesome
Like yer so 'wicked kewl' Johnny Boy


THE LIGHT LAUGHTER OF SIXTEEN SEVENTEEN EIGHTEEN

eLatEd aNd imMOrTAL

B U T   I N   A   D A R K E R   C O R N E R   A W A Y   F R O M   T H E   O T H E R S

YE DONE ROIGHT
YE DONE ROIGHT
FOIGHT HIM LATER
STRATEGY
YE DONE GOOD SON DONE GOOD
KUSTHI
KUSTHI

A S   S O O N   A S   H E ' S   O U T   O F   E A R S H O T

AN EMBARRASSMENT
TO ME
TO HIS BROTHER
TO HIS NAME

M Y   F O O K I N '   N A M E

A N   E M B A R R A S S M E N T   T O   M Y   N A M E

*to my name ...*

T H E   Y O U N G E R   F I R E ' S   L A U G H T E R   T E A R S   T H R O U G H   H I M

IT RIPS HIM
HE KNOWS THEY'RE LAUGHIN' AT HIM
HE KNOWS WHAT THEY'RE SAYIN'
THE PRETTY GIRLS AN' THAT HALF-BREED

G A D J E   F O O K I N '   C H A V O

GORJA

H E   S T A R E D   A T   H I S   F I R E   W H I C H   B E C A M E   T H E I R   F L A M E S

Is me skirt wicked cool? Or just wicked?
What's 'Maureen Maureen the Jackeen Queen'?
That's yer ma 'tis her name - her title
What's it mean?
Slang fer a person from Dublin - it rhymes is all
She's American
Trust me after that fight - ya won't never hear it again
Didn't yer da teach ya any Traveller words - any Shelta or Gammon?
It's complicated
How so?
Said he was from Galway
Ya didn't know?
Wait - so what's coachie?
Culchie
Like cultured - like posh - like fancy?
Fancy means really likin' someone like a crush - like love

LIKE DO YA FANCY ME BOSTON ?
I FANCY YA JOHNNY BOY

HER FACE IN THE FIRELIGHT
THE TIME OF IT

THE TIME OF THIS MOMENT
JUST A LITTLE MORE TIME

wait ...

HE BOLTS OVER TO MIKEY THE PIKEY BIKEY

CLIPS TWO CANS

RETURNS TO HER
RETURNS TO HER

HE RETURNS TO HER
IT MADE HIM FEEL SO GOOD TO RETURN TO HER

HE REFLECTED ON THAT AS DEEPLY AS HE COULD
IN THE QUICKNESS OF THAT MOMENT THEN LEANS AND FINDS HER EAR

let's go ...

SHE FLASHES BLUSHING CHEEKS AND EYES TO BLACK MARIA

Don't do anythin' I wouldn't do
Yeah but ya would

*yes i would ...*

Gorja & Pavee Lackeen

*boston irish*
*they says yer not even irish*
*says ya ain't us*
*not even really american neither*
*call ya half-breed*
*gadje*
*i call ya gorja like my uk cousins say*

*sounds like gorgeous*

*yer da had character - i seen the pictures - but ya got yer looks from yer ma*
*she's class too - proper class*

*lace curtain from the states*

*yer beautiful like her i have never seen such a beautiful boy*
*yer eyes yer skin yer lips*
*ya'd get a tan if the sun was ever out*
*the shape of you*
*yer all lean sleek an' well formed an' yer from america*

*america*

*american boy yer settled but yer wild in a way*
*yer not really a traveller then*
*just enough to unnerstan' me though*
*i'm the prize here*
*they all wanna marry me*
*marry me off*

*offerin' - offerin' t'ings that i do not want*
*an' i won't have it never*

       *NO NAY NEVER*
       *NO NAY NEVER NO MORE*

*y'know that one then doncha?*

*god yer all lips an' eyebrows*
*súile deas*
*look that up or ask around ...*

*cheek bones*
*torso*
*chestnut curls*
*yer hands*
*yer hands*
*the face on you boy*

*the face on you*

*kiss me - are ya goin' to kiss me?*

*gypsy girl*
*red cascade curls*
*pretty face*
*so young for the age in the look of your eyes*

*like mine in a way*

*skin*
*your pale pale skin*
*the smell the taste the touch of it*
*the lightness of your freckles*

*the legs on you girl*

*the legs that run you around - as you absolutely do not give a fuck*

*about any of this*
*about my dad*
*about who we are*
*about what he did - or that we're here now*

*you like my mom*

*she likes you too*

*and she hates the travellers*

*kissing your neck - kissing your lips*
*the hotness of your mouth*

*the shiver of your body's quiver my breath is hot on your shoulder*
*you've got goosebumps*

*i've got butterflies ...*

*butterflies*

*every time i hear you*
*every time i'm near you*
*every time i think about you*
*every time i see you*
*every time i hope to see you*
*which is always*

*always*

*i'm sick with it*
*i'm light with it*

*it gets me high this fluttering*

Dreams In America

BY A FIRE IN A FIELD UNDER STARS TOGETHER ALONE

i love you
i love you boy
i love you girl
always love you boy
always love you girl
always and in all ways

WHEN THIS IS OVER I'M TAKING YOU WITH ME

TAKE ME TO AMERICA
AWAY FROM ALL OF THIS
I WANNA LIVE IN AN APARTMENT WITH A DOORMAN
IN A PROPER CITY WITH THE TALL TALL BUILDIN'S

skyscrapers

NEW YORK CITY

wait

i want the cable cars - san francisco
i thought you wanted to act?
tá
los angeles?
they can send me great big fat chauffeur car
london?

NO THEY'VE TRAVELLERS THERE

WASTERS CHANCERS DOSSERS
THEY COULD FIND ME
WE'RE GOIN' AWAY FROM HERE - FROM ALL OF THIS - FAR FAR AWAY

kiss me - kiss me again

what do ya want fer yerself?
dunno
ya don't then do ya?
they kinda - one day the cops and fbi came and took my world away
they even took my trophies
that's mad
don't ya want nothin' fer yerself - fer the future?

HISEYESBATHEINSTARLIGHTDRINKINGITBREATHINGIT

i want you

HERSTOMACHFLUTTERSSHEGASPSASSHEHEARSIT

come see me tomorrow i know a place

shE wHispeRed in hEr kiSs

She Said I Know A Place

Here



You'll need the wellies
Wellies?
Muck boots for the mud n' rain
Mud and rain?
Hapes
Hapes?
A lot
You mean heaps?
It's what I said
Heaps of mud and rain? Some place
Don't be wise



Can ya drive a motorbike?
Think so
Ya t'ink ?
I had a little Honda 50 mini-bike
Can ya drive that t'ing then?



Where'd you get that?
Loaner from a friend



Oh is it?
Isn't yer da some scarface feckin' drug lord?
Ya can borrow a bike fer a minute



FLATTENS OUT A TEN PUNT NOTE ON IT

Got a pen?
Tá

HE WRITES DIRECTLY ON THE MONEY

*BACK IN A FEW - JOHNNY & LOA*

FOLDS THE BILL IN THE SCARF LIKE A LETTER - TIES ITS ENDS IN A LOOSE KNOT

HUNTS - FINDS A NAIL

PALMS IT INTO THE TREE
HANGS MIKEY'S MONEY-NOTE IN LOA'S SCARF

Yer slick then very polite
I'm not stealing Bike Mike's bike
Y'know he stole it from someone else from somewhere?
Yeah but without it - he'd just be Mike
Fair play
You take the helmet - I got the goggles

Q U I C K   K I C K   T O   T H E   S K I N N Y   V I N T A G E   B I K E

SHE PURRS

I  MEAN  SHE  REALLY  FUCKING  PURRS

A N D    T H E Y    G O

THEY  GO  GO  GO  GO  GO

OUT OF THE TRAVELLER CAMP
OUT AWAY INTO THE MIST
THE FOG
THE CLOUDS AND WET GREEN HILLS OF IRELAND

I    R    E    L    A    N    D

THE FRESHEST WETTEST AIR YOU'VE EVER BREATHED
THE FRESHEST WETTEST AIR YOU'VE EVER SMELLED

SMELLED LIKE HOME

A N D   T H E Y   W E N T   A N D   W E N T   A N D   W E N T   A N D   W E N T   A N D   W E N T

R A N    O U T T A    G A S

PUSH HER TO THE PETROL STATION
CAUGHT IN THE RAIN
HID OUT IN THE PUB
HOT BURGERS COOL NOT COLD PINTS

SHOTS AND STORIES

K I S S I N G A L M O S T F U C K I N G I N T H E B A T H R O O M

HANDS ALL OVER

H I P S   L I P S   F I N G E R   T I P S

THE SHINE OF YOUNG THEM IN THE BATHROOM MIRROR
IN ALL THE WINDOWS AND GLASSES

R E F L E C T E D

IN AND OFF OF ALL THE BOTTLES

OFF THE GIANT ETCHED MIRRORS

TWO  BEAUTIFUL  PEOPLE  MADLY  IN  LOVE

IN THE SHINE OF THEIR OWN LIGHT
IT LIT THE ROOM
SPARKED EVERY SURFACE

HE  TIPPED  LIKE  AN  AMERICAN

THE RAIN LET UP
THE OLD LADIES BLUSHED AT THE LOVE THEY WITNESSED
HE RAN FOR THE BIKE TUCKED 'ROUND THE BACK OUT OF THE RAIN

He's very handsome and the accent – is he a posh boy from London?
He's an American
Oh, he's an American

IT  WAS  STILL  COOL  TO  BE  AN  AMERICAN  BACK  THEN

Well have a lovely afternoon
I will we already are
He's very handsome
Tá he is ya said that
It bears repeatin' lassie

AND  THEY  WERE  OFF  AGAIN

GOING

THE HILLS THE TARMAC THE GRAVEL ROADS THE HARD-PACKED DIRT THE

*S h E e p !*

THEY  SKIDDED  SLIDD-ED  AND  SKIDDED  SOME  MORE

Sheep crossin' it's a t'ing here

THE LAUGH AND LILT OF HER VOICE

THE  SING-SONG  MUSIC  OF  HER  SPEECH

THE CLOSENESS OF HER FACE TO HIS

HER BREATH ON HIS NECK

ITS WARMTH

HIS  DELICIOUS  SHIVER  CHILLS

Hey move sheep move ...

NIL

Please?
Ya never been caught behind a flock of sheep before?
No, how do we get them to move?
Ya don't
What do you do?
Ya wait

T H E Y   W A I T

   *THE WAITING IS THE HARDEST PART*

THE BIKE IDLES SHE JUST HOLDS HER FACE TO HIS NECK NOTHING IS SAID

B A R K I N G   D O G S   A N D   F A R M E R S
F I N A L L Y   M O V E   T H E   F L O C K

Afternoon
Afternoon

AND OFF AGAIN
AND OFF AGAIN

THE RIDE
THE TRAILS
THE PATH

T H E   C O A S T

AND ON
AND ON
AND ON
AND ON

johnny cut down this trail by the river

H E R   S O F T   V O I C E   J U S T   E N O U G H   T O   H E A R

AND THEY SLOWLY RIDE
HER ARMS HIS RIBS
HER HIPS
HER LEGS AROUND HIM

T H E   M A G I C   O F   T H E I R   H O L D I N G

ONTO THE BIKE
O N T O   E A C H   O T H E R

THEY SWAY IN THE MOTION OF THEIR TRAVEL
T H E I R   S L O W   M E A N D E R   D O W N   T H E   P A T H

TO THE PRIVATE PLACE SHE KNOWS
I N   S I L E N C E   T H E Y   R I D E   A L L   T H E Y   H A V E   I S   E A C H   O T H E R

A L L   T H E Y   N E E D   I S   H E R E

NOTHING TO BE SAID

J U S T   B E   J U S T   F E E L

JUST BEING AND FEELING THE TOGETHERNESS OF SELF AND OTHER
THE BEAUTY OF BEING YOUNG AND IN LOVE WITH SOMEONE WHO IS JUST AS IN LOVE WITH YOU
THEY RIDE IN THIS FEELING FOR MILES

T H E Y   R I D E   I N   T H I S   F E E L I N G   F O R   M I L E S

take a right she whispers

HE GENTLY SLOWS AND TURNS UP THE LITTLE PATH
SLICING UP THE HILL
JUST BEHIND THE WOODED GLEN
OFF THE RIVER BANK

A   T U N N E L   O F   T R E E S   A   B E E C H   G R O V E

OPENS TO A CLEARING
SOME OLD SHACK - JUST THE FRAME WITH A ROOF
UNDERNEATH IT
INSIDE IT

A   G I A N T   C A N V A S   T E N T

Is that some sort of archaeology tent?
T'ink so, from the military surplus

W A I T   H E R E

S H E   D I S E M B I K E S

W H I C H I S N O W A N D F O R E V E R M O R E A N D A L W A Y S A N D E V E R A W O R D

HELMET OFF
TOUSLED HAIR
THE RED OF IT
THE RED OF HER TOUSLED HAIR

S H E   K I S S E D   H I M   W I T H   A N O T H E R   W A I T   H E R E

SHE CHILLS HIS NECK WITH A CLOSE YER EYES - HOOKS AN OLD CAR BATTERY TO SOME

O P E N

C H R I S T M A S   L I G H T S

This is my place then do ya like it?
It's beautiful
Help me build a fire?

C ' M E R E   T O   M E   B O Y

kiSs me

Klimt

D A N A E

K L I M T

T H E   L O V E R S

THE PALE HER SKIN
THE RED HER HAIR
HER SLEEPING BLISS
HER SLEEPY WAKE
THE GOLD THE GOLD THE GOLDEN GLOW THE LIGHT OF DAWN
THE FLICKER FLICKER GOLDEN LIGHT IN THE MIST
THE STILL-BURNING EDISON GLOW JUST ENOUGH TO BE SEEN IN THE DIFFUSED SUN
THE HORIZON WAITS THE DAY BEHIND THE ROLLING FOG
THE MIST OFF THE COAST
OFF THE RIVER
INLAND IT IS DAY ALREADY
BUT THE OCEAN WIND HOLDS COAST CLOUDS CLOSE

C O C O O N I N G   T H E M   T H E R E

THE SMOKE ORANGE GLOW OF THEIR FIRE WAFTS OUTSIDE THE HIDDEN TENT
HER HIDDEN TENT
HER PLACE
HER SPECIAL PLACE
HER CAMP AWAY FROM CAMP
HER PLACE TO ACT AND SING

A  P L A C E  T O  R U N  A N D  H I D E  A  P L A C E  T O  D A N C E  A N D  D R E A M

she had her radio there

h e R   c a s s e t T e S

THE FAINT GOLD LIGHT SOMEHOW KISSES THEIR TABLEAU
REFLECTED OFF THE WORN SOFT ONCE ROUGH WOOL ARMY BLANKET
HER OFF-WHITE BEDSPREAD GLOWED WITH GOLD
THE GOLDEN LIGHT OF THEM
THEIR LOVE
THEIR SLEEP ENTWINED
THEIR HIDING IN THIS GOLDEN PLACE
LIGHT LIKE GOLD LEAF PAINTS THE TREES THAT BOTH HIDE AND KEEP THEM
THE GOLDEN SLUMBER OF THE REDHEADED GIRLS IN KLIMT'S PANTHEON
DANAE
MERMAID
LOVERS
TREE OF LIFE

their actual beech grove

T H E  G O L D E N  F O R E S T  T H E  G O L D E N  S T A R S  F L I C K E R  F L I C K E R

OFF THEIR BLANKETS
INSIDE THEIR TENT

hey lo'
hey yerself

HEY LO
HEYLO

H A L O

THE GLASS CANDLE GLOBE BEHIND THEM CASTS ITS LIGHT AROUND HER

B E A T I F I C

you're covered in light
you are my light

T H E Y   S T A Y E D   T H E R E   A N D   H I D   T H E R E

AND LIVED THERE
AND LOVED THERE
ALL WEEKEND

I N   E A C H   O T H E R ' S   L I G H T

yEr tellin' mE aboUT   j o H n N y

b o y  -  yoU knOw - NiL - alL of iT

Johnny Boy & Loa

T H E   S E C O N D   A N D   H I S   S O N

What the fook is goin' on da?
What are ye on about?
People are talkin' da
About what?
About Johnny Boy
We don't talk about Johnny Boy
Yer tellin' me what's going on
Nothin's goin' on
Did ya send Joe's fat fook nephew to the states?

yer tellin' me the whole fookin' thing

Joe found Johnny Boy
So he's alive?
Aye
It's
It's what?
An' yer goin' after him?
Johnny Boy?

T H E   T I M E   P R E S S E S   H I M

Da why'd ya send Fatty?
This is Joe's thing
He does nothin' without ya
Joe hates him - hates him deep
Why though?

da it's like ...

Like what?

like he knows ...

Knows what?

THAT JOE KNOWS
THAT JOHNNY BOY KNOWS
THAT JOE HATES HIM

That's not news

N I L

YER NOT HEARIN' ME - IT'S LIKE JOHNNY BOY KNOWS THAT JOE REALLY HATES HISSELF

H I M S E L F

HIS VERY OWN SELF MORE THAN HE HATES JOHNNY BOY

Yer sayin' Joe hates Joe?
Exactly

Joe hates Johnny Boy
It's deeper than that an' ya know it
Aye he hates him deep I said

T H A T ' S    M E    W H O L E    P O I N T

JOHNNY BOY KNOWS
THAT JOE KNOWS
HE HATES HIMSELF
MORE THAN HE HATES HIM
MEANIN' JOE HATES JOE MORE THAN JOE HATES JOHNNY BOY

T H E    L O O K

It's bad blood I said
Why?
That I can't tell ye
Ya have to
Cannot
Someone better
Why?

because i got a terrible feelin' ...

T H E    T I M E    H A N G S    C L A U S T R O P H O B I C

Johnny Boy beat him
Beat Joe?
Aye we don't speak of it
Aye but they are now
Who?
They're all talkin' about it - but no details - nothin' as to why

*secrets don't stay*

Johnny Boy whipped Joe?
Aye
Beat him good?
Indeed he did
Took him apart?
Aye
When he was a kid?
Aye
In a proper bare-knuckle the whole clan an' all an' everyone?
Nay it was diff'rent

*tell him just enough*

IT WASN'T A FAIR FIGHT - WASN'T UNFAIR NEITHER
BUT IT WAS JUST
IT WAS PERSONAL

An' he was a kid - seventeen?
Just eighteen - it's terribly important to Joe that we know that

HE   WAS   EIGHTEEN   AN'   A   LEGAL   MAN

EVEN THOUGH WE'S AIN'T SUPPOSED TO KNOW ANY OF IT
EVEN THOUGH WE ALL KNOW
EVEN THOUGH WE'S THERE

E V E N   T H O U G H   W E   S E E N   I T   W I T H   O U R   O W N   E Y E S

AT LEAST MY GENERATION SEEN IT
HE MAKES A BIG POINT A' MAKIN' SURE WE ALL KNOW THAT

An' skinny?

A Y E

WHIP-THIN WIRY
THIN AN' FIT
NOT SKIN AN' BONES LIKE THEY SAYS
STRONG SWIMMER
RAN TRACK
AN ATHLETE
BODY OF A DANCER
HE COULD MOVE
HIS DA'S PROPER HARD ON HIM
TOO MUCH THEY SAYS
MADE HIM HARD

An' he whipped Joe?

H U M I L I A T E D   H I M

COULD HAVE KILLED HIM
HE HELD BACK
JUST TO LET EVERYONE KNOW

Know what?

T H A T   H E   W A S   T H E   M A N   -   H E   W A S   T H E   B U S I N E S S

*that should be enough ...*

Does that answer the question?
Nil

H E   D U C K S   I N   S O F T L Y   S L O W L Y

DA - WE ALL KNOW HE WHIPPED HIM
AN' IT WAS BAD
AN' JOE'S SEEKIN' REVENGE
AN' IT 'S BEEN BURNIN' HIM
EATIN' HIM ALIVE ALL THESE YEARS

An'?
Joe's old man now - auld fella

So?
He's almost old then
So?
So he can't win

SO  HE  CAN'T  WIN

*so he can't win ...*

*it was so strange to hear it put that way*

*so simple - so true*

AN'  HE'S  A  RIGHT  FECKIN'  CHEAT  IN  A  FIGHT

Mind yerself?
Fook sake da!

C  A  N     H  E     F  O  O  K  I  N  '     W  I  N  ?

NO

So this is a setup?
Life's a set up
Fair play

B U T

But what?
Why?
Revenge that's why I told ye

B    O    L    L    O    C    K    S    !

*his eyes he sees ...*

JOHNNY BOY WHIPPED HIM
IT ERODED HIS POWER
HIS POSITION
HIS STANDIN'
THAT'S WHY HE WANTS HIS REVENGE

I ' V E    T O L D    Y E    A    T H O U S A N D    T I M E S

Y A    T O L D    M E    F U C K    A L L    !

I've enough of this
Ya feckin' tellin' me
I need to go
I need to know
Ye'll know the back a' me hand!
Ya's goin' fookin' nowhere!

HE  GRABS  A  FIST  OF  JACKET  AND  TWISTS

PULLS HIM TO HIS PLACE BY HIS LEATHER

Y E R   T E L L I N '   M E   T H E   R E A L   T H I N G   D A

THE THING WE NEVER TALK ABOUT
NOT THE ONE WE NEVER TALK ABOUT BUT TALK ABOUT
THE THING WHAT'S BEHIND IT

T H E   O N E   W E   N E V E R   E V E R   T A L K   A B O U T

I've no time for this!
Yer me da, an' somethin' foul is about to happen
Let go of me!
Yer the only person who knows that's ever gonna tell me
Knows what son?
The truth
What truth?

T H E   T R U T H   O F   W H Y   T H E Y   F O U G H T   I N   T H E   F I R S T   P L A C E

PURPLE RED HATE SCARLET SHAME RAIDS HIS FACE BETRAYS HIM

B E T R A Y S   T H E   M A N

BETRAYS THE TRUTH
BETRAYS HIS POSITION
BETRAYS A LIFETIME OF KEEPING JOE'S SECRETS
THE SECRETS OF THE CLAN

B E T R A Y S   I T   A L L   T O   H I S   S O N

*because some blood is thicker than others ...*

T H E   T I M E   C L O S E S   A R O U N D   H I S   T H R O A T

HIS HOT BREATH BURNS - WHISPERING HIS SECRET POISON

loa

What?
Loa
What's Loa?
Not what who
Right then who's Loa?
In the car off to the pub
I'm not feckin' off to the pub until ya tell me who's this Loa!

*can't fookin' breathe ...*

In the car off to the pub an' I'll tell ye

*someone needs to know ...*

I'll tell ye every goddamned thing there is to know

A HOLLOWED MAN SAID HE'S BUYING

Fook sake yer buyin'?
Aye
Ya's alright da?

HIS SON CAN'T FIND HIS EYES

Da?

*i can't even look at him*
*can't breathe*
*can't talk*
*i slip into the gammon*

krosh de rog ...

get the car

the blaupunkt played an '80s song it brought him back brought it all back in that same way songs can kill you

Of Lasses & Horses

T H E   V A N N E R   H O R S E   R A N   T H E   F I E L D

LOA FOLLOWED SHE DIPPED AND TWIRLED
SHE TWISTED TURNED
SHE WANTED TO BE AN ACTRESS THE ONLY OTHER LOVE WAS HER HORSE
AS SHE DANCED BESIDE IT
SHE WOULD SPIN AND TWIST AND TURN AND TURN AWAY AGAIN
ELATED

A G A I N   A G A I N

THEY CURLED EACH OTHER 'ROUND

THE TRACE OF HER HAND MUSCLED HAUNCHES
HIPS & HOCKS
THE WIND IN HER HAIR ITS MANE
THEIR FEATHERED HEELS
THE BEAUTY OF THEIR PALENESS

R I C H N E S S   O F   T U R F

THE FLIGHT OF HER SMILE

C I R C L I N G   A L L   A R O U N D   E A C H   O T H E R   I N   T H E I R   D A N C I N G

pat pat there there

PURE WHITE GHOST VANNER HORSE
PURE WHITE GHOST TRAVELLER GIRL

S H E   D R E A M E D   O F   T H E   F A I R   A N D   D A N C I N G   A N D   M U S I C

CARTS RACING
BOYS FIGHTING
FLIRTING FAWNING
CALLING HER DEADLY

T R Y I N G   A N D   F A I L I N G   T O   B U Y   H E R   H O R S E

    'TIS NOT FER SALE
    CAN WE BREED IT THEN?
    NEVER


J O E   S P I E D   T H E M   A C R O S S   T H E   F I E L D

C O V E T O U S

THE MOST BEAUTIFUL GIRL
THE FINEST LASS

A N D   M O R E O V E R

THE MOST BEAUTIFUL HORSE

THE FINEST HORSE

IT WAS RIGHT THEN AND THERE HE DECIDED

HE WOULD OWN THEM BOTH

AND SHOW THEM OFF

NEXT GYPSY FAIR
EVEN TO THE BIG UK ONE EVEN
HE'D SHOW 'EM OFF ALL RIGHT

HE WOULD SHOW THEM ALL

THEN THEY'D KNOW
THEN THEY'D SEE

I SAW IT AS A PORTENT
A WAKING DREAM
SHE WAS MAKING FRIENDS WITH

THE ACT OF DANCING WITH

HER WHITE HORSE

PRACTICING
INVOKING IT

SUMMONING

MANIFESTING IT

THE SYMBOLS & SIGNS ARE EVERYWHERE

THE PATTERNS AND THEIR MEANINGS
IF YOU CARE TO SEE THEM

IT WAS THE LAST BEAUTIFUL MORNING OF HER LIFE

BOTH JOE AND I COULD SEE IT
SHE DANCED AWAY HER LAST TRUE MORNING
PRANCING IN ECSTASY WITH HER ALL-WHITE VANNER HORSE
TOWARDS THE END SHE MOUNTED IT

BAREBACK

NO SADDLE
NO REINS
SHOCK OF WHITE HAIR THROUGH FINGERS LACED ITS MANE

NOW WOVEN TOGETHER THEY ARE

ENTWINED
SHE LEANED FORWARD ALMOST LAYING

F E E L I N G

ITS SKIN
ITS BREATH
ITS SINEWS
ITS MOVEMENT

A N D   T H E   B E A T I N G   O F   I T S   H E A R T

SHE JUST HUGGED IT AND RODE IT SLOWLY 'ROUND THE FIELD

K N O W I N G   N O T   T H A T   T O M O R R O W

HER LIFE WOULD NEVER BE THE SAME

song ends as the kid parks it he knew what he'd have to say maybe he wouldn't have to maybe

The Pub

A   N I C E R   P U B   T H A N   Y E ' D   H A V E   F E C K I N '   E X P E C T E D

ANY GARBAGE WHISKEY
PINTS PINTS
BEER N' A BALL
SPIT-WARM CANS - SOME USED AS ASHTRAYS
CRISP PACKETS AN' THE LIKE

B A R M A N   S H R I E K S

O I   T I N K E R   T H E   F E C K I N '   F L A S K !

Ye's don't serve the poitín!

*laughter*

Ye's made that one?
Aye

hmmm a quandary - he thinks on it ...

Roight then boyo give us a rip!

P A S S E S   F L A S K

HE RIPS HIS SNORT - THEY CHEER AN' IT'S SORTED

D A Y L I G H T   H A T E S   D A R K   B A R S

TAUNTS IT
SEEKS THE CRACKS
WARMING GLASS OF WINDOWS
THIN LINES CUT BORDERS OUT OF SHADE
WINDOWS FRAME IT

A S   T H E   L I G H T   A L W A Y S   D O E S   I T   C U T S   I T S   W A Y   I N

D A Y L I G H T   C U T S   D A R K N E S S
ROCK PAPER SCISSORS

T H E   D A Y L I G H T   T H E   W O R L D   A L W A Y S   W A I T S
OUTSIDE THE BARS

there's something beautiful about drinking in the afternoon

B E A U T Y   I F   B Y   C H O I C E

MOROSE IN THE MORNING
MORE SO IF YOU MUST
PATHETIC IF BY HABIT
TRAGIC IF YOU'RE THERE BEFORE THEY OPEN
WAITING

*S h a K i N g*

tWiTcHiN'

HOPING HE'LL CASH THE CRUMPLED FOLDED CHEQUE
and maybe let you keep some today in spite of the tab

ELEVEN IN THE MORNING

LOSERS
DRUNKS
DAY DRINKERS
TINKERS
PENSIONERS
THE LOST
THOSE SEEKING


THOSE THAT ARE IRREPARABLY FUCKED

ONE THIRTY IN THE AFTERNOON

FIVE PAST THREE

THEN LATER AT DUSK WHEN THE SUN FINALLY RUNS

WHEN THEY'VE SURVIVED THE LIGHT
ONCE AGAIN

THEY PROP THE DOOR OPEN TO LET OUT THE SMOKE

So?
So
So?
I bought 'em like I said
Now yer tellin' me all of it
Aye, son the whole story
Who's Loa?

HE SAID HE'D SAY
HE SAID HE'D BUY AN' PAY
NOW HE'S DONE THAT

NOW HE HAS TO

HE TURNS CRANES SCOPES SPIES

We're goin' to the booth
Huh?
The banquette ye hear me?
Yeah sure foine foine foine

THEY SCOOP SCRAPE GRAB PINTS CANS CRISPS

ONE LAST GOOD RIP BEFORE THEY CAP CUFF POCKET THE FLASK

AND MOVE INTO THE BOOTH LIKE THEY JUST ROBBED A BANK

# What the fook is all this secrecy?

*the drama the drama always the drama*
*they're right about that*
*travellers always the drama - always an angle*
*it's feckin' exhaustin'*

H I D I N '   L I K E   T I N K E R   T A I L O R   S O L D I E R   S P Y

*jaysus just tell the boy*
*let it off yer chest man*
*for christ's sake*
*he's just lookin' at me*

Y A ' S   A L R I G H T   D A   ?

FER REAL
YA DON'T LOOK WELL
LET'S GET YA SOME AIR

*just say it ...*

# Da?

*say it*

# Da can ya hear me?

*now or never bang down a shot an' say it ...*

# Da!

SHOT
B A N G
GLASS
S L A M
PINT
G L U G G A   G L U G   G L U G
AHHH
S L A M

M O U T H   T O   S L E E V E

LOA IS JOE'S NIECE
SHE WAS
SHE AN' JOHNNY BOY WERE YOUNG AN' IN LOVE
WHEN HE WAS OVER HERE MEETIN' HIS TRAVELLER SIDE
HIDIN' OUT

J O E   D I D N ' T   L I K E   I T

DID NOT LIKE IT ONE BIT

D I D N ' T   L I K E   J O H N N Y   B O Y

SAYS HE'S FROM TOWN
CITY BOY

G A D J E
outsider non-traveller

C A L L E D   H I M   H A L F - B R E E D

YANK - AN' HE DIDN'T LIKE THE ATTENTION HE GOT NEITHER
HANDSOME AN' HE COULD FIGHT

H A T E D   H I S   M A

SHE COULD SEE RIGHT THROUGH ALL OF IT
ESPECIALLY JOE'S SHITE
REMEMBER SHE WAS MARRIED TO BIG JOHN

J O H N N Y   A C E

IT ALL STARTED TO ADD UP TO JOHNNY BOY LOOKIN' LIKE HE'S THE MAN

H E I R   A P P A R E N T

YOUNG AS HE WAS
JOE'S A BUFFOON BUT HE AIN'T THAT STUPID

H E   C A N   B E   A   C U T E   F E C K I N '   H O O R   W H E N   H E   N E E D S   I T

HE COULD SEE THE WRITIN'
THIS BOY'S THE UNDERCOVER ALPHA
HE THREATENED JOE
HE DIDN'T ACTUALLY THREATEN HIM MIND YE
IT THREATENED HIM
ALL OF IT
AN' YE SEE
HERE'S THE THING

T I M E   S L O W S   H E   H U N C H E S   C L O S E   T O   H I S   K I D

C'MERE TO ME SON

H E   D O E S   T H E N   I N   Q U I C K   W H I S P E R S

the quickest of whispers - like if whispers could whisper

SON YE KNOW THE TRAVELLER CULTURE
WITH THE MARRIAGES AN' THE ARRANGED
SO UH JOE BEIN' THE CHIEFTAIN
THE HEAD OF THE CLAN
DECIDES
HE'S GONNA MARRY LOA OFF
THAT STARTED IT ALL
LIT THE FUSE

HE FADES HANGING HEAD SITTING HUNCHED

THE WEIGHT

THE WEIGHT OF CARRYING THIS
THE WEIGHT OF HOLDING IT

THE PRESSURE

THE BURDEN OF BEING THE ONE TO SAY IT

AN' JOE
BIG JOE
BIG FOOKIN' JOE
JUST LOOMIN' OUT THERE OVER HIM HER US
EVERYWHERE AN' ALWAYS THERE
CASTIN' HIS SHADOW OVER THE WHOLE SHITE FOOKIN' WORLD WE LIVE IN

Who'd he marry her off to?
Himself

FOOK SAKE

JOE FANCIED HIS NIECE AS IT WERE

FOOK SAKE DA

AN' UH AS UH – I DON'T KNOW
A POWER THING
CONTROL
DOMINANCE?
JEALOUSY?

HE GOT OUT OF LINE WITH HER GOT A BIT ROUGH AN' HE UH

HE SHAKES CONVULSES GASPS
HE CRIES IN THE PUB WHERE THEY KNOW HIM

TEARS
is spelled the same as tears

IN FRONT OF HIS OWN SON

HE GAGS AS HE GRASPS THAT THE SAYING OF IT

ALOUD
the saying of it allowed

IS GOING TO CHANGE REALITY

LIKE IT WAS NEVER REAL BEING HIDDEN LIKE THAT

HE UH
JOE HE UH

JAYSUS

*i can't say it ...*

W H I S P E R   I F   Y O U   H A V E   T O

he raped her

T H E Y   S I T   I N   T H E   T I M E

he raped his niece

T H E   T I M E   S L O W S   A N D   S I C K E N S

BECOMES SICK

H I S   V I L E   W O R D S   A   P O I S O N

JOHNNY BOY BEAT THE SHIT OUT OF HIM - LIKE THE YANKS SAY
ALMOST KILLED HIM
PROBABLY WOULD HAVE

H A D   T O   P U L L   T H E   S H O T G U N   O N   H I M

HE LOOKED LIKE HE WAS GONNA RIP THE THING OUTTA ME HANDS
SNAP IT IN HALF

A N '   K I L L   M E   W H E R E   I   S T O O D

HE WANTED HER TO GO TO AMERICA WITH HIM EVEN AFTER WHAT HAD HAPPENED

T H E   S I C K   T I M E   S L O W S

HE FELT LIGHT HAVING SAID IT

L I G H T E R   N O T   B E T T E R

SHE FOUND SHE WAS PREGNANT
I DONE ME JOB TO MAKE SURE SHE'D BE STAYIN'
JOE MARRIED HER AN' BOUGHT HER A BRAND NEW CARAVAN
TOP LINE TOURER
DIDN'T MATTER
SHE DIDN'T CARE

I T   W A S   A   P R I S O N

SHE STARTED TO DIE IN THERE

T H E   S I C K N E S S   O F   T I M E

LATER SHE RAN OFF WITH ANOTHER BUNCH OF TRAVELLERS
IT'S COMPLICATED - THERE'S MORE TO IT THAN THAT
THEN SHE RAN FROM THEM TOO
SHE'D BEEN RUNNIN' EVER SINCE - IN ONE WAY OR ANOTHER

DRINK DRUG THAT'S JUST OTHER FORMS A' RUNNIN' AN' HIDIN'
THING IS SHORTLY BEFORE WE SEEN JOHNNY BOY ON TELE AT THOSE FIGHTS

S H E   K I L L E D   H E R S E L F

AN' IT IS MY PROFOUND BELIEF
THAT JOHNNY BOY IS COMIN' FOR REVENGE

H E   I S   G O N N A   K I L L   J O E

P I N C H E S   T H E   S N O T   O F F   H I S   N O S E   N '   W I P E S   I T   O N   H I S   L E G

JOE'S THINKIN' HE'S THE MASTERMIND LURIN' JOHNNY BOY TO A TRAP
THE TIMIN' IS TOO MUCH OF A COINCIDENCE
JOE SAYS THERE'S NO COINCIDENCES
I'LL GIVE HIM THAT ONE
THE MAN'S A BROKEN CLOCK

T H E   W H E E L

Y'KNOW THE WHEEL ON THE ROMANI FLAG THE GYPPO FLAG?
IT REPRESENTS THE WAGON
THE WHEEL
MOVEMENT
TRAVEL
BUT IT COMES FROM INDIA THEY'VE IT ON THEIR FLAG TOO
SPINNIN' WHEEL
WHEEL OF KARMA
WHEEL OF TIME

W H E E L   O F   P A I N

K A R M A

WHAT GOES AROUND COMES AROUND
AN' IT'S COMIN' AROUND
WHAT YE DONE IS WHAT YE GET

R E A P   W H A T   Y E   S O W   T H A T ' S   T H E   B I B L E   T H A T   O N E

I SHOULD HAVE LET HER GO

D R I N K S   H I S   B A C K W A S H E D   H A L F - C R U S H E D   C A N

BUT I'M LOYAL
I'M A LOYAL FOOL

H E   Q U I C K S   A   S H O T

THE HEAVY GLASS BOTTOM OF A PROPER OLD-SCHOOL SHOT GLASS SLAPS THE TABLE

*nice people son*
*normal people son*

HE COULDN'T SAY IT SO HE THOUGHT IT
HE OFFERED UP

D E C E N T   P E O P L E   S O N

A N D   L E T   I T   D I E   I N   T H E   A I R

*decent people don't do these things*
*decent people don't live this way*

M I G H T   H A V E   B E E N   T H E   R E S T

SLEEVE WIPES TEARS

H E   Q U A F F S   H I S   K I D ' S   F L A T   P I N T

SLEEVE TO MOUTH AGAIN
HE SNIFFS THE BACK OF HIS HAND TO SUCK HIS SNOT AND TEARS

W H A T   T H E Y   S A Y S   A B O U T   U S   I S   T R U E   W E ' R E   S A V A G E S

HE GAGS AND STUMBLES OUT THE BOOTH
SHUFFLE RUNS OUTSIDE BENT AT HIS WAIST
IN A CONE OF YELLOW LIGHT
THAT PAINTS HIM AS SICK AS HE IS

H E   P U K E S

H E A V I N G   S H A K I N G   C O N V U L S I N G
HE THROWS UP THE LAST OF IT

T H E   B I L E
THE LINING OF HIS STOMACH

F I N A L L Y   C A T C H I N G   B R E A T H   A N D   S P I T T I N G

S P I T T I N G   S P I T T I N G   I T   U P

T H E   L A S T   O F   T H E   P O I S O N   H E   C A R R I E D   I N   H I S   G U T S

EVERYTHING HE'D DONE
EVERYTHING HE HADN'T

The Black Maria

SHE'S A BOHO FOOKIN' PRINCESS

LIKE THE NIGHT
DARK SEDUCTIVE INVITIN' DANGEROUS
AN' SHE'D AN EYE FOR JOHNNY BOY

EVERYGIRLHASAFRIENDWHOWANTSTOFUCKHERBOYFRIEND

> *DON'T FALL IN LO-OVE*
> *SHE'S A BEAUTY*
> *SHE'S A ONE IN A MILLION GIRL*
> *ONE IN A MILLION GIRL*
> *WHY WOULD I LIE-I-I?*
> *NOW WHY WOULD I LIE?*

Ya like that song Johnny Boy?
Yeah
Don't fall in love it's warnin' ya
Too late
Ya fallen then?
Yes

CAN I TELL YER FORTUNE ?

READ YER PALMS?
SEE YER FUTURE?
TEA LEAVES?
TAROT CARDS?
CAST THE BONES?

*come to me wagon ...*

I'VE A CRUSH ON YA SINCE WE MET SINCE WE KISSED

I thought you were friends?
We are that's why I'm stayin' away I love her lots but I fear
Fear what?
Come let me read ya

SHE TAKES HIS HANDS HIS LONG FINGERS

SHE TRACES THE LINES ON HIS HANDS

*his love line is broken - two loves ...*

LOSS

*don't tell him never tell him ...*

VENGENCE
REVENGE
THEN VICTORY

A VICTORY WITHOUT JOY

A DESERT PLACE
SHE LOSES HERSELF
A THEFT - SHE STEALS?
NAY
SOMETHIN' IS STOLEN FROM HER
NO

S H E    I S    S T O L E N

A WOMAN
A BEAUTIFUL WOMAN - BRUNETTE

You?
Nay, yer ma
My mom?
Aye, she's a spell on her in a way
This isn't cool

S H E    W A K E S

SHE WAKES AN' TAKES YA HOME

H        O        M        E

T H E    W O R D    S L A P P E D    H I M    L I K E    H I S    F U C K I N G    D A D

*where's home?*
*there is no home*
*they took it*
*the house the cars*
*the college money*

E V E R Y T H I N G

IT'S WRONG FOR YA TO BE HERE
IF YA STAY THERE'LL BE DEATH
IF YA GO THERE'LL BE DEATH
IF YA RETURN THERE'LL BE DEATH

W H E N   Y A    R E T U R N    T H E R E    W I L L    B E    D E A T H

People fucking pay you for this?
This ain't the fair, we shine it up fer the punters - the buffers
What about Loa?

D A R K N E S S

This isn't funny
I'm not jokin'
What about me and Loa?

Y O U ' L L    B E    A P A R T

TWO PATHS DIVERGE

IT'S TRAGIC

Y O U ' R E   H E R   F U C K I N G   F R I E N D

YOU TELL ME YOU'RE CRUSHING ON ME
THEN YOU 'MAGICALLY' SEE THAT WE BREAK UP?

Johnny she's my best friend my only friend my age - our age

J O H N N Y   S O M E T H I N '   P O W E R F U L ' S   A B O U T   T O   H A P P E N

When?
At the end
Fuck this
Wait

P L E A S E

AGAIN SHE TAKES HIS HANDS

there's a choice ...

P L E A S E   B E L I E V E   M E   P L E A S E   B E L I E V E   M E

YA CAN TELL YER MA TO LEAVE NOW
RIGHT NOW

T O D A Y

AS SOON AS YA CAN
IT'LL SPEED HER WAKIN'

A   W   A   K   E   N

TO THE TRUTH THE TRUTH OF WHAT I SEEN
YA CAN LEAVE AN' BE SAD ON A MISSED ROMANCE
BUT IT'LL BE JUST THAT
REGULAR SAD
THEN YOU'LL BE GONE AN' T'INGS WILL HEAL
AN' GO BACK TO AS THEY WERE INTENDED

H E   S H A K E S   I N   T H E   T I M E

OR YA CAN STAY AN' WATCH IT ALL PLAY OUT
THE DEEPEST LOVE YOU'LL EVER KNOW
IT'LL CHANGE YA FOREVER
IT'LL CHANGE THE CLAN
ALL OUR WORLDS

B U T   I T   W I L L   E N D   I N   T R A G E D Y

P L E A S E

IT'LL HAUNT YA

CRIPPLE YA IN A WAY
IT WILL TIE YER LIFE TO THIS SUMMER
TO THESE EVENTS
TO US FOREVER
AN' NO ONE'LL BE HAPPY

T H E   S H A L L O W   O F   H I S   B R E A T H I N G

Is there something you can do?

*i'm doin' it now ...*

JOHNNY I JUST SEE THE FUTURE
IT ISN'T SET BUT THESE ARE THE LIKELIEST OUTCOMES

I   S A W   Y O U   A T   T H E   F A I R

DOING THINGS
THE BLESSINGS
THE SPELLS
PROTECTION
WITH THE CUSTOMERS

A girl's gotta make her money
So it is all fake!

T H E R E   I S   R E A L   M A G I C K   J O H N N Y

AN' I COULD HELP YA
I COULD TRY BUT

P L E A S E

JOHNNY I'VE ALREADY SEEN MORE N' I SAID

I   H A D   A   D R E A M

IT WAS A VISION

A   T E R R I B L E   V I S I O N

An' there's
There's what?

T H E R E ' S   T H I S   O T H E R   A S P E C T

I CANNOT TELL YA
BUT I WANT TO
I WANT TO TERRIBLY

D E S P E R A T E L Y

Tell me
I can't

Tell me
I don't wanna hurt anyone
This is just Traveller bullshit
I'm sorry I should have just told Loa
Then why didn't you?

SHE'S ME ONLY FRIEND JOHNNY

IT'S ALL OLD WOMEN GROWN MEN AN' BABIES HERE
I DIDN'T WANT TO RUIN THIS SUMMER SHE'S HAVIN'
SHE'S SO HAPPY

I NEVER SEEN HER SO HAPPY

SO RUIN MINE?
HUH?
HAD TO RUIN SOMETHING?
JEALOUS?

A Y E

YES
NO
MAYBE I AM
I TOLD YA 'CUZ YA WILL BE LEAVIN'

THAT MUCH IS CERTAIN

I WANT TO SAVE YA THE PAIN AN' LOA
THERES'S SO MUCH PAIN AN' LOSS FOR HER ON THIS PATH
FOR YA BOTH
ESPECIALLY HER

YOU SAID IT WAS A BEAUTIFUL LOVE

IT IS

SHE BEGINS TO SOFTLY CRY

*and it cannot last ...*

STOP IT NOW
PLEASE TELL YER MA TO TAKE YA HOME
I'M NOT PLAYIN' WITH YA
I'M NOT DOIN' IT TO BE SELFISH
IF YA COULD SEE WHAT I SEE JOHN

D O N ' T

I KNOW ONLY YER MA CALLS YA JOHN

What's the this other aspect that you can't tell me?

I  C A N ' T

YA WON'T BELIEVE ME
YOU'LL HATE ME AN'
IT WAS STUPID
I THOUGHT

I  S H O U L D N ' T  H A V E  D O N E  I T

*i'm sorry ...*

P U T  I T  O U T  O F  Y E R  M I N D

*i'm sorry ...*

I T ' S  S T U P I D  I ' M  P R O B A B L Y  W R O N G

*i'm  sorry ...*

I JUST THOUGHT
I SEEN SOMETHIN' BAD
AN' THOUGHT YA'D BE STRONG ENOUGH TO HEAR IT
YER SOLID IN THE READIN'S
ALMOST TOO STRONG

*i'm sorry*

I just thought I'd save Loa
Save Loa?
Some heartache is what I meant

S H E  C A N ' T  B E  S A V E D

*nothin' can save her*

I SHOULDN'T HAVE SAID ANYTHIN'
CLEARLY THIS WAS A MISTAKE

You don't think that
My sayin' it was the mistake

*if ya could only see ...*

I ' L L  A S K  M E  M U D D E R  A N '  M E  A U N T I E S

THEY'RE MORE POWERFUL
BETTER AT INTERPRETIN'
I SEE MORE BUT THEY DECODE IT BETTER
THE IMAGES ARE NOT ALWAYS WHAT THEY SEEM

What images?

D E A T H  J O H N N Y

death everywhere an' ...

A N D    W H A T  ?

*don't say it*

A N D    W H A T  ?

*don't say it - ya have to*

A N D    W H A T  ?

an' we end up together

SHE KISSES HIS HANDS
HER FLUTTERING LIPS
HER TEAR-STREAKED FACE

H E    H O L D S    H E R    E Y E S    W I T H    H I S

SHE PEELS OFF HER SHIRT
H E R    B L A C K    L A C E    B R A

HE THUMBS AWAY HER TEARS AS MANY AS HE CAN
T E A R S    D R Y I N G    O N    H E R    F U L L    L I P S

HER DARK CURLS
H E R    S P A N I S H    E Y E S

HER OLIVE SKIN
K I S S    M E    L I K E    W E    K I S S E D    A T    T H E    F A I R    T A K E    M E    H A V E    M E

HE CRADLES HER FACE WITH BOTH HIS HANDS
S O F T L Y    B R U S H I N G    H E R    T E A R S    B R U S H I N G    T H E M    A L L    A W A Y

SHE COMES TO KISS HIM
S H A K I N G    B R E A T H L E S S

HE LEANS TO HER CARESSES HER HAIR SLOWLY TUCKING IT BEHIND HER EAR
T H E H E A T O F H I S B R E A T H O N H E R S K I N T H E C O O L T H O F H E R T E A R S

HIS LIPS TRACE THE PATH OF HER TEARS BRUSHING HER NECK HER TEAR-STAINED CHEEK UP TO HER EAR
H I S S I N G    W H I S P E R E D    W O R D S    T H R O U G H    H I S    T E E T H

fuck you

# Betrothed

A L L   S U M M E R S   E N D

We're leaving
What?
We're leaving
Why?
Because of all this shit
What shit?

T H I S   T R A V E L L E R   S H I T

IT'S ALL SHIT
IT'S FUCKING BULLSHIT JOHN

But Loa
You love her?

the shy nod of uh uh yeah and if you make me say it i'll fucking cry

That's why we're leaving
Because I love her?
Because of Joe
What are you talking about?

W E   A R E   L E A V I N G   B E C A U S E   O F   J O E

BIG FAT FUCKING FULL OF SHIT
HE'S JEALOUS

J E A L O U S

JEALOUS OF YOUR DAD
NOW HE'S JEALOUS OF YOU
HE'S PULLING HIS TRIBAL CARNY FUCKING GYPPO BULLSHIT
BECAUSE YOU LOVE LOA

What?

B E C A U S E   S H E   L O V E S   Y O U

What tribal bullshit?
They arrange marriages when they're kids - you know that
And?
He's saying she's betrothed to him
She told me she wasn't promised or arranged to anyone ever
Her parents say different
Since when?
They say since always, but really since last night
What the fuck?
It's shit John

E V E R Y T H I N G   H E R E   I S   A   L I E

THIS WHOLE WORLD

THEIR WORLD THE TRAVELLER THING

IT'S BULLSHIT BABE YOUR DAD ESCAPED IT

AT LEAST THAT'S THE LIE I TOLD MYSELF

HE DESPISES THEM - HE COULDN'T GET OUT FAST ENOUGH - BUT IT'S ALL HE KNEW
YOU CAN TAKE TO BOY OUT OF THE CARAVAN BUT YOU CAN'T TAKE THE CARAVAN OUT OF THE BOY

but you love him?

HE'S IN FUCKING PRISON

WE ALL ROMANTICIZED THIS MYTH - THE MYTHOLOGY OF HIS LIFE

*of this lie*

It's pulling scams and rigging bare-knuckle fights

*i was asleep*

It's stealing

*i was blind*

It's statutory rape

*now i am awake and i will protect my son*

IT'S CHILD BRIDES
THEY TREAT GIRLS LIKE CATTLE
LIKE SHEEP

LIKE PROPERTY

Where is she?
With Joe and her family ironing out the deal
The deal?

HE'S BUYING HER

what the fuck?

What do you think this is babe?

HE BECAME UNTETHERED FROM THE TIME

The girls are like property

      *TRUTH HITS EVERYBODY*
      *TRUTH HITS EVERYONE*

LOA'S MOM CAME TO ME LAST NIGHT
SHE LOVES YOU

I'M SORRY
I'M SORRY FOR YOU BOTH

T H E S E   M E N   -   T H E   O N E S   W I T H   T H E   P O W E R

JOE AND HIS LOT

T H E Y   F E A R   Y O U

What did I do?
It's what you could do
You mean the fight? They - it was - they came after me!

I T   D O E S N ' T   M A T T E R

YOU HAVE AN EDUCATION WAITING FOR YOU
COLLEGE STARTS IN THE FALL

A N D   Y O U   A R E   G O I N G

I DIDN'T WANT TO COME HERE IN THE FIRST PLACE
YOU TOLD ME IT'D BE AN ADVENTURE - LIKE CAMPING
DAD SAID HE WAS FROM FUCKING GALWAY

T H I S   W A S   Y O U R   I D E A

I T   W A S   M Y   M I S T A K E

I   D I D   E V E R Y T H I N G   Y O U   F U C K I N G   S A I D

I   W I L L   N O T   F A I L   Y O U   A G A I N

We are going home
I have to see her
They won't let you
There's no way
They're going to announce it tonight around the fire

T H I S   I S   H O W   T H E Y   L I V E

AND YOU ARE A THREAT TO THAT WAY OF LIFE
YOU COULD TAKE THIS OVER
YOU COULD BECOME LIKE THEM

O R   W O R S E   L I K E   Y O U R   F A T H E R

YOUR DAD WOULD HAVE LED THIS
BUT HE TOOK A TRIP TO BOSTON FOR A DRUG DEAL
TO START SETTING THINGS UP
THE DRUGS

T H E   G U N S

WHAT GUNS?

THE IRA BABE
PURPLE SHAMROCK
BLACK ROSE

rōisín dubh

A L L   T H O S E   B A R S   J O H N

HE WENT TO BOSTON AND HE NEVER CAME BACK
HE'D SEND THEM MONEY
DO SOME DEALS WITH THEM
BUT HE WAS USING THEM FOR A PLACE TO HIDE IF HE EVER NEEDED IT
ONE DAY HE DID

A R E   T H E Y   L O O K I N G   A F T E R   U S ?

PROTECTING US?
OR KEEPING US CLOSE BECAUSE YOUR DAD SAID?

B E C A U S E   H E   P A I D   T H E M ?

MAKE SURE I'M NOT NEAR THE BOSTON OFFICE OF THE FBI?
MAKE SURE I DON'T FUCK ANYONE WHILE HE'S AWAY?

*i can't breathe - my face feels numb ...*

I know it hurts babe
How could she?

S H E   D I D N ' T

THE PARENTS OWN THE KIDS
THEY SELL OR TRADE THE MARRIAGE RIGHTS
THESE POOR GIRLS
IT'S BARBARIC

S H E   N E V E R   H A D   A   C H A N C E

SHE CRADLES HIS FACE WITH HER HANDS
A   B E A U T I F U L   W O M A N   N O W   T H U M B S   H I S   T E A R S   A W A Y

I ALLOWED MYSELF TO GET SWEPT UP IN HIS WORLD
WHEN YOUR DAD GOT ARRESTED I GOT SCARED
HE TOLD ME IT WAS FOR OUR SAFETY
BUT IT'S SO HIS COUSINS CAN KEEP AN EYE ON ME

I   W A S   W R O N G

I WAS WRONG ABOUT THIS
I WAS WRONG ABOUT YOUR DAD
I LET HIM RAISE YOU AS HIS SON IN HIS WAY - WHILE HIDING THE TRUTH OF HIS PAST
I LIED TO YOU ABOUT WHO HE WAS AND WHAT HE DID THE SAME WAY I LIED TO MYSELF

I   L E T   H I M   H I T   Y O U

I LET HIM HIT YOU
I LET HIM BEAT YOU

W H E N   Y O U   W E R E   A   J U S T   A   L I T T L E   B O Y

SHE COULDN'T SAY THE REST

*a little boy*
*trying to protect me from him - from him hitting me*
*and i never left him - i never left*

*was i scared?*
*was it the money?*
*is that how he bought me?*
*is that how i let him buy me?*

Mom, why are you crying?
We're going back to Boston
I'm not going
You are
You can't stop me I'm eighteen

H E   T R A I L E D   O F F   ' C U Z   H E   K N E W

There's nothing for you here
I'm taking her with me

the soft exhausted tears of knowing you cannot win

C R A D L I N G   H I S   F A C E   A G A I N

I AM SORRY FOR ALL OF THIS
BUT THIS EVENT

T H I S   ' M A R R I A G E '

she spits it bitter

THIS ISN'T LIFE
I WON'T PRETEND IT
YOU HAVE TO LET HER GO

I F   H E   T O U C H E S   H E R   I ' L L   K I L L   H I M

THAT'S WHY WE ARE LEAVING
WE ARE LEAVING NOW
BEFORE THEY ANNOUNCE IT
WE'LL BE GONE

T H I S   I S N ' T   F A I R

SHE HANDS HIM HIS TICKET

Life's not fair

The Fire

AROUND THE FIRE FAT JOE BEAMING HIS BELLY FULL

loa

LIP QUIVER TEARS OF SHAME EYES DOWN

*don't look don't look don't look don't look at them*
*don't look at them lookin' at ya like that*
*like they knew*
*like they won*
*like ya aren't better than them*
*they always knew*
*ya were too good of a get*
*too fine a prize*
*fer joe to let ya go*
*he'd keep ya fer himself*
*that's why no betrothal as a child*
*like the others*
*he wanted to get a fine look at me*
*see if i grew up pretty*
*sexy*
*fit or fat?*

*tits & teeth to the top of the line*

*don't cry don't cry*
*don't let them see ya cry*
*just let the hat brim cover yer eyes*

*look to the sky maybe ya can pray*
*to jesus the black madonna the fairies an' all the pagan saints*

*oh fook i'm cryin'*
*cry me a feckin' river*

*johnny where are ya why'd you leave?*
*ya left 'cuz yer ma knew*

*me mudder told her straight*

*an' that's how it is*
*there's how it is an' there's how it ought to be*

*this is how it is*

*our life our ways are the law of the land here*

*yer ma is from town so beautiful an' smart*
*city girl - college - uni*
*everythin' i want fer myself*

*wanted*

*she finally wised up an' took ya home*

*the familiar taste the salt of my tears*
*on my lips*
*the cool burn as they stream*
*drain down my neck*
*i hadn't cried all summer*
*forgotten yet familiar*
*the last familiar t'ing*

*nothin' will ever be the same – never be like it was*

*everythin' is different now*

*it can't be this*
*it can't be this*

JOE

ON THE LITTLE BULLSHIT STAGE HE HAD BUILT FOR THIS

So we have an announcement to make

HE GRABS TO HOLD HER HAND – SHE SLIPS IT – HE TAKES HER WRIST

*his gross fat fook old man hands*
*the hand he jerks off with – fookin' hateful cunt*

'Tis a glorious day I'm foinally t'be settled!

SILENCE

T H R O W S   H I M

H E   R E A L L Y   T H O U G H T   T H E R E   W O U L D   B E   M O R E   C L A P P I N G

SO LOOK HERE NOW
LOA THE BEAUTY OF OUR TRIBE
THE FOINEST GIRL WE EVER SEEN
WELL WE DONE SAT DOWN WITH HER MA AN' HER DA
AN' WE DONE THE ROIGHT T'ING THE ALLIANCE OF TWO GREAT FAMILIES THAT'LL KEEP OUR CLAN GOIN'
FER THE FUTURE

H E   G R A B S   H E R   W R I S T   A N D   R A I S E S   I T

AS IF SHE WON A BOXING MATCH

she's his fookin' niece ...

FROM THE CROWD IN AND AS HISSING WHISPERS SOME MOUTH IT SILENT

O T H E R S   S A Y   I T   W I T H   A N D   I N   T H E I R   E Y E S

JOHNNY BOY

W A T C H E S   F R O M   T H E   D A R K   B E H I N D   T H E   T R E E S   E D G E   O F   C A M P

STOLEN MOTORBIKE

I D L I N G

THE BLACK MARIA

S I L E N T L Y   F L O A T S   B E S I D E   H I M

She's with child
Right
It's yours
Fuck off you're lying

L E A V E   T H I S   P L A C E   T H E R E   I S   N O T H I N '   F O R   Y A   B U T   D E A T H

I'll kill him
That's the death I mean an' more
Then it's fate I'm supposed to
Not yet
Not yet?

Y O U   M U S T   L E A V E   -   F L Y   F R O M   H E R E

FIND THE LIGHT
FIND THE SUN
FIND THE OCEAN

T E A R S   S T R E A M   D O W N   H I S   C H E E K S

*i love her so much ...*

HE WANTED TO WHISPER
BUT HE COULDN'T
SO HE JUST LET HIMSELF FEEL HIS TEARS EVAPORATE
AND DRY TO THE SKY
LIKE THE WORDS HE LACKED
LIKE THE WORDS HE HOPED
LIKED THE WORDS HE'D PRAY IF HE BELIEVED
AND HE WANTED TO BELIEVE
BUT HE COULDN'T
HE ALREADY KNEW TOO MUCH

L E A V E   T H I S   P L A C E

FROM THE LITTLE JOKE OF A STAGE

So Loa an' me are betrothed!

HE REALLY THOUGHT THEY'D CHEER

We been seein' each other fer some toime now ye may not know

*don't say it*
*don't say it*

*he's gonna say it*

T H E   G I R L   I S   W I T H   C H I L D   !

*they know it's johnny boy's*
*they know ya know it too*
*ya sick fuck*
*what are ya gonna do - raise his beautiful child?*
*what happen when it looks like him?*
*what then?*

JOHNNY BOY

F L I C K S   H I S   F O O T

THE BIKE SLIPS INTO NEUTRAL ENGINE OFF

S L O W   R O L L S   D O W N   T H E   G E N T L E   S L O P E   F R O M   T H E   T R E E S

SILENTLY
R O L L S   C L O S E R

QUIETLY
I N   T H E   D A R K

HE KICKS HER ALIVE PURRING FLICKS THE SWITCH

H   E   A   D   L   I   G   H   T

FAT FACE
T H R O T T L E   B A C K   H A R D   I N   N E U T R A L

S H E   R O A R S

F A T H A N D F A T F A C E S Q U I N T S T U R N S H I D E S F R O M T H E L I G H T

Ahh who's that turn off the feckin' boike!

LOA

H E R   S T R A W   H A T   B R I M   L E V E L S

SHE STARES INTO THE LIGHT
THE PATH OF HER TEARS CATCH IT REFLECT IT WET SPARKLE STREAKS OF SHAME
SHE NEVER WOULD HAVE THOUGHT
SHE HADN'T DARE DREAM IT

*he came for me*

*i can't believe it ...*
*he came for me*

JOHNNY BOY THOUGHT TO LAUNCH THE BIKE AT JOE
N O T   S U R E   W H Y

LATER HE REMEMBERED MICKEY ROURKE LAUNCHED A BIKE AT A MOD PILL-HEAD IN THE MOVIE RUMBLE FISH
TO  SAVE  HIS  BROTHER  RUSTY  JAMES

BUT HE DIDN'T REMEMBER IT THEN
SO  HE  WASN'T  SURE  WHY

HE JUST REVVED THAT THING IN THE DARK
SAYING  NOTHING

FLICKER LIT BY THE FIRE

Hey now someone tell that – is dat Mikey? Who the fook?

> *MY BOYFRIEND'S BACK*
> *AN' YA GONNA BE IN TROUBLE*

Fook sake – turn the feckin' bike off

> *HEY LA*
> *HEY LA*

HE STEPS OFF THE STAGE

WALKS  STRAIGHT  IN  TOWARDS  THE  BIKE

THROTTLE TWIST

CLUTCH  POP

LAUNCH  THE  BIKE  AT  REDLINE  RPMS

NICE BIG FAT TARGET STANDS RIGHT IN FRONT OF YOU
COMES STRAIGHT IN
LIKE AN IRISH GYPPO BOXER

HITHIMLIKEAMETALROCKET

WHILE  HIS  CLAN

HIS TRIBE OF BARE-KNUCKLE-FIGHTIN'
SHITE-TALKIN' TOUGH GUYS

JUST  STOOD  AN'  WATCHED

NO ONE CAME TO HIS AID
NO ONE DID ANYTHIN'

BECAUSE  IT  WAS  SHOCKIN'  AN'  UNUSUAL ?

ULTRAVIOLENT

PERHAPS

AN' BECAUSE LIKE ANY FIEFDOM

ANY DICTATORSHIP
THEY ALL SECRETLY HATED JOE

AN' WANTED HIM DEAD

THEY WAS A LITTLE UNSURE AS TO THE BIKE THOUGH

BUT THIS WAS PERSONAL

MIKEY

DEFINITELY THOUGHT

*guess i'll be stealin' meself another motorbike*

THE REAR WHEEL KEPT SPINNIN' ALL DUTCH-ANGLED IN THE DIRT
BUZZIN' LIKE A SAW THAT JUST CUT DOWN THEIR MAN

JOE

GASPIN' GRASPIN'

AW FOOK FOOK FOOK
AHHHH ME LEG ME RIBS
BOYS BOYS GET HIM COME ON BOYS GET THE
AHHHH FOOK
CAN'T UH BREATHE UH
ME FOOKIN'

UNGHHH

ME 'EART ME 'EART

HE HAD A SNAPPED LEG
BROKEN RIBS
AN' WAS HAVIN' WHAT LATER WAS CONFIRMED TO BE A MASSIVE HEART ATTACK

JOHNNY LOOMED OVER HIM

SKINNY TEENAGE AMERICAN DEATH

Get up

HE COULDN'T
SO JOHNNY BOY KICKED HIM IN HIS SHATTERED RIBS
WITH HEAVY MOTORCYCLE BOOTS

KICK KICK KICK

BOYS BOYS
ME 'EART ME 'EART
FOOK FOOK NO NO WAIT
JOHNNY BOY JOHNNY BOY
WAIT WAIT

JOHNNY BOY

P L E A S E   P L E A S E

GRASI GRASI

K I C K   K I C K

MIKEY

*those are me boots!*

W E W A T C H E D H I M K I C K J O E N E A R L Y T O D E A T H

*he does wear them well ...*

H E   K N E W   H E ' D   B E   N I C K I N '   A N O T H E R   P A I R

JOHNNY BOY KICKED THE SHIT OUT OF HIM

L I T E R A L L Y

HE KICKED HIM AN' KICKED HIM
IN THE GUTS
UNTIL HE SHIT HIS PANTS
WHICH WAS ACTUALLY A SYMPTOM OF THE HEART ATTACK
AN' QUITE COMMON AT THAT

W E   D I D N ' T   K N O W   T H A T   A T   T H E   T I M E

THE STORY LIVES ON FOREVER
AS JOHNNY BOY LITERALLY KICKIN' THE SHIT OUT OF BIG JOE
KICKED HIS FACE
BROKE HIS JAW

T H E N   T H E   P A R T I N G   S H O T

C O U P   D E   G R Â C E

WE ALL JUST WATCHED

J O H N N Y   B O Y   P U L L E D   O U T   H I S   C O C K

AN' PISSED ON JOE
LOOKIN' AROUND AT EVERYONE WATCHIN' EVERYONE JUST LOOKIN' AT HIS

B E A U T I F U L   C O C K

PISSIN' ON THE LORD OF THEIR LIVES

Y E A H   Y E A H   T H I S   I S   Y O U R   L E A D E R   S A I D   H I S   C O C K

HE PISSED STRAIGHT IN JOE'S FACE WHICH WOKE HIM UP
SO JOE'S LAID OUT HAVIN' A HEART ATTACK

BUSTED UP GASPIN' FOR AIR
AN' HE'S GETTIN' A MOUTH FULL OF PISS
CHOKIN' ON IT
DROWNIN' IN IT

C L U T C H I N '   H I S   C H E S T   T A L K I N '

    ME 'EART
    ME JACKET
    ME MEMBERS
    ME MEMBERS

FRETTIN' ABOUT HIS 'MEMBER'S ONLY' AS HE'S NEARLY DYIN' WHILE ANOTHER MAN'S MEMBER

I T   F E C K I N '   W R I T E S   I T S E L F

**IT WAS BRUTAL**

HE SLOWLY SCANNED THE TRIBE
FINISHES IT UP SHAKES HIS COCK
LAST DRIPS AN' DROPS HE DOESN'T RUSH THIS AT ALL
COCK IN HAND

Y O U   C A L L   T H I S   M A N   Y O U R   K I N G ?

SAID THAT COCK

S H A K E   C A L M   S H A K E   S H A K E

PUTS HIS COCK BACK IN HIS PANTS
BUTTONS HIS JEANS
HE RIGHTS THE BIKE

L O A   R U N S   T O   H I M

T H E Y   S T A N D   I N   T H E   H O T   S T A R K   F I R E L I G H T

ITS  CRUEL  SHADOWS

S H E   H O L D S   H E R   H A N D   T O   H I S   C H E S T

THE BOYS AN' SOME KIN ATTEND TO JOE
GET HIM ON HIS FEET
HE'LL NEED THE HOSPITAL SAYS ONE OF THE JUNIORS

F O O K   H I M !

FROM THE CROWD

THE OTHER JUNIOR GETS INCENSED AN' STARTED TEARIN' THROUGH THE CROWD AT WHO MIGHTA SAID IT

C O U L D   H A V E   B E E N   A N Y O N E

JOHNNY BOY GRABBED A JAR OF POITÍN

O U R   M O O N S H I N E   H I G H - P R O O F   A L C O H O L

THROWS IT SMASHIN' AGAINST JOE'S CARAVAN
HE FLICKS A BRASS ZIPPO AN' FLINGS IT

*an' me feckin' zippo!*

MIKEY ADDED IT TO HIS LIST

J O E ' S   C A R A V A N   E X P L O D E D   I N T O   F L A M E S

JOE HAD A HABIT OF SOAKIN' HIS HANDS IN PETROL
TO TOUGHEN THE SKIN FOR THE FIGHTS
SO HE ALWAYS HAD PETROL ON HAND - SO TO SPEAK
HE ALSO SMOKED LIKE A CONVICT
THE FACT THAT THIS HADN'T HAPPENED ALREADY IS KIND OF A MIRACLE

J O H N N Y   B O Y   B E A T   T H E   G Y P S Y   K I N G

AN' BURNT HIS CASTLE DOWN - WAS IT A FAIR FIGHT?

N I L   F A R   F R O M   I T

BUT WHAT THEY WERE FIGHTIN' ABOUT WEREN'T FAIR TO BEGIN WITH
ALL'S FAIR IN LOVE AN' WAR

A N '   T H I S   W A S   L O V E   A N '   W A R

I   P U L L E D   O U T   T H E   S C A T T E R - G U N

BOTH BARRELS LOADED

I F   A N Y O N E   F O L L O W S   U S   S A I D   H I S   C H I N   F L I P

H I S   E Y E S

I WANTED TO TELL HIM I BELIEVED HIM AN' WE WOULDN'T
BUT I COULDN'T GET IT OUT

    J U S T   G O   S O N   G O

ALL I COULD MUSTER
HE RODE OFF LIKE A DEMON IN THE NIGHT

T E E N A G E   D E A T H   G O D   A V E N G I N '   A N G E L

ON A STOLEN BIKE
IN STOLEN BOOTS
WITH A PREGNANT TRAVELLER GIRL
WITH ONE COACH TICKET FROM SHANNON INTERNATIONAL AIRPORT
TO BOSTON LOGAN

FOR A FLIGHT THAT

HAD ALREADY LEFT

An Garda Síochána

T H E   G U A R D I A N S   O F   T H E   P E A C E

FOR ALL THE TALK
FOR ALL THE BILE
FOR EVERY STORY
FOR EVERY TALE OF HARASSMENT

D I S C R I M I N A T I O N

V   I   O   L   E   N   C   E

SHAKEDOWNS HATE CONDESCENSION

D E R I S I O N

O P P R E S S I O N

FOR ALL THE BITCHIN' AN' MOANIN'
SONGS OF WOE

B I G   J O E

T H E   H E A D   O F   T H E   T R A V E L L E R S
THE OUTSIDER MORE OUTSIDE THAN THOSE OUTSIDE THE OUTSIDE

C A L L E D   T H E   P O L I C E   F O R   H E L P

AN GARDA SÍOCHÁNA

T H E   G U A R D I A N S   O F   T H E   P E A C E
WERE WAITING FOR THEM AT SHANNON INTERNATIONAL AIRPORT

T H E Y   C O U L D   F E E L   M E   H A N D   I N   I T   T H E Y   K N E W   I   W A S   C L O S E

CONDUCTIN' IT
ORCHESTRATIN' IT
THEY EVEN TOOK THE BIKE BACK FOR ME

but loa

LOA

WITH HER LAST DOSE OF HEART AND CHARM
HER LAST MAGIC SMILE

S A Y S

NAY THAT'S NOT TRUE
MIKEY LOST THAT BIKE TO HIM IN A BET OVER THE FIGHT
FAIR N' SQUARE
HE'S JUST A LYIN' PIKEY TRYNA STEAL HIS BIKE BACK IS ALL

W E   A R E   T O   A R R E S T   H I M   F O R   A S S A U L T   W I T H   A   D E A D L Y

I T ' S   A   L I E   S H E   L I E D

IT WAS JUST BARE-KNUCKLE
THEY'RE SOUR GRAPES
ON ACCOUNT OF JOE GETTIN' PUT IN HOSPITAL

Y E R   S A Y I N '   T H I S   K I D   T U N E D - U P   B I G   J O E ?

AN' WON THE BIKE IN A BET OVER THE FIGHT?
AN' THE REST IS JUST TRAVELLER SHITE?

H E ' S   T H I N K I N '

Aye, 'tis what exactly happened
An' yer sixteen then is it?
Tá - yes
That's your ma?
Aye, that's me mudder

H E ' S   L I K I N '   T H A T

BECAUSE HE HATES TYPIN' UP PAPERWORK
AND ALSO - FUCK THE TINKERS

R I G H T   L E T ' S   G E T   A   L O O K   A T   T H I S   K I D

YOU

YER THE YANK?
YER MEANT TO BE OFF ON A PLANE?

Yes sir
Ticket

SHOWS

You've missed it
I'll pay the fee - next one out
What'll you do with that motorbike?
They've got long term parking
And?
I'll pay for that then come back and

YOU WON'T BE COMING BACK

I'll have it shipped

THE KEYS

HE TRIES TO WAIT

T H E Y   G O T   H I M

*they got me*

HE'S HAD  -  THE CUT DEAL  THUS

SHE GOES HOME
HE GOES HOME
HE HANDS THE KEYS
THEY TAKE THE BIKE

## ON YOUR WAY

THEY RUSH TO EACH OTHER

AND HOLD
AND KISS
AND CRY
AND WAIT
AND WAIT

HE DOES HIS BEST TO KISS UP ALL HER TEARS

ALL HER TEARS

he couldn't speak

SHE GAVE HIM HER STRAW HAT

he wore her scarf

THE INEVITABILITY OF TIME

TIME

THE EVER CONSTANT UNRELENTING INDIFFERENT

WRATH OF TIME

A NICE ENOUGH YET OFFICIOUS FEMALE GARDA BREAKS IT

HAS TO

ITS' HER JOB
BESIDES IT'S LATE
AND ALSO - FUCK THE TINKERS

THE SOUND OF HER SCREAMS

GO SON NOW
RUN FOR THAT GATE AND DON'T COME BACK

THE SOUND OF HER CRIES  THE SOUND OF HER CRIES

JOHNNY BOY I LOVE YOU

I LOVE YOU
I LOVE YOU

HER VOICE ECHOED IN HIS HEAD ALL THE WAY TO THE GATE

TO THE WASHROOM
TO THE PUB
TO THE PLANE
TO THE RUNWAY

THROUGH THE SKY

ALL THE WAY TO BOSTON

HER VOICE ECHOED IN HIS HEAD FOREVER

and ever
and ever
and ever

AMEN

Romany Brown

S H E   K I L L E D   T H E   B A B Y

A   B   O   R   T   I   O   N

ENDED THE PREGNANCY
GOT RID OF IT
TOOK CARE OF IT

an' i can't say i blame her

J O E   W E N T   M A D

I T   W A S   H E L L   F O R   H E R   T H A T   G I R L

SOMETIME LATER THERE'S THIS SONG FROM
THE ADDICTION & THE PORNOGRAPHY PYROS OR SOMEBODY
GOES LIKE

> *CURSED TO BE BORN*
> *BEAUTIFUL POOR AND FEMALE*
> *THERE'S NONE THAT SUFFER MORE*

T H A T   L I N E   -   T H A T   L Y R I C   R I G H T   T H E R E   S T U N G   M E

THE FOOKER' COULDN'T REALLY SING THOUGH
VERY NASALLY VERY REEDY
BUT THEM'S THE FOLKS FROM TOWN ALL THE ELECTRONIC GUITARS AN' THE SYNTHESIZERS
NO FIDDLES NO SQUEEZE BOXES
BUT HE FECKIN' KNEW WHAT HE WAS SINGIN' ABOUT

he waits

J O E   B E A T   H E R

H E   H U R T   H E R   B A D

WE GO BY THE OLD WAYS - WITH THE OCCASIONAL BACK OF THE HAND WHEN NECESSARY

B U T   I T   N E V E R   R E A L L Y   I S

JOE'S THE CHIEFTAIN HE'S THE MAN
I'M THE SECOND
HIS LIEUTENANT
HIS CONSIGLIERE
HIS FIXER
HIS ADVISER
THE ONE WHO SPIES THE MODERN WORLD
HIS CONDUIT TO THE OUTSIDE WORLD

T H E   W O R L D

AN' THAT WORLD IS EVER CHANGIN'

T H A T   W O R L D   O F   T O W N

IT'S WHY WE DESPISE IT
WHY WE DENY IT

W H Y   W E   F E A R   I T

DESIRE IT

T H E Y   T H E   O T H E R

OTHER WORLD
OTHER WAYS
NOT OUR WAY BUT THE YOUNG FOLK THEY SEEK IT TO SOME DEGREE
THE STUFF THE CLOTHES MOSTLY
THE PRETTY DRESSES
THE FINER THINGS

N I C K I N '   N '   S T E A L I N '

THE DRESSES
THE TRAINERS
TRACK SUITS
THE HIP HOP
THE RAP STYLE
GOLD CHAINS
NOW NICKIN' A GOLD CHAIN IS STILL NICKIN' A GOLD CHAIN
YER NOT SELLIN' USED TRAINERS IN A JAM
BUT A TRADE OF A GOLD CHAIN CAN SETTLE THINGS

G O L D

G O L D   C A N   G E T   Y E   O U T   O F   A   J A M

TRAINERS IS MONEY MIND YE
BUT A GOLD CHAIN CAN FIT IN YER POCKET
SMALL PORTABLE VALUABLE FOR A TRADE

T R A D E

J O E   T R A D E D   L O A   T O   O L D   R O M A N Y   B R O W N

GOT HIMSELF A DIVORCE
THERE'S NO DIVORCE IN IRELAND AT THAT TIME
AN' NO ONE'S EVER LEGALLY MARRIED ACCORDIN' TO IRISH LAW BACK THEN

J U S T   T O   U S

OLD WAY A HAND-FASTIN' WHICH CAN BE UNTIED
HE'D TREATED HER CRUEL
HE BROKE HER
HE BROKE HER HEART
HER SOUL
HER BODY

H E R   T E E T H

HE   BROKE   HER   BEAUTIFUL   TEETH

THAT SMILE SHE HAD
LOA COULD LIGHT UP A ROOM
THE WHOLE CAMP
HURRICANE LOA
THE TWIRLIN' GIRL
SHE LOVED TO DANCE AN' SING
DESIGNED HER OWN CLOTHES
AN ARTIST'S SOUL IF EVER I SEEN ONE
SHE WANTED TO BE AN ACTRESS

HE   TORE   HER   DOWN   LIKE   HE   TORE   DOWN   HER   FORT

IT'S AN AWFUL THING TO GET WHAT YE WANT - AN' REALISE - WANTIN' IT

## DOES NOT MAKE IT WANT YE BACK

BUT   HE   HAD   THE   POWER   AN'   THAT'S   HOW   HE   USED   IT

IT GOT THEM BOTH NOTHIN'
BUT YEARS OF PAIN
WASTED TIME
NO GOOD CAME OF IT
NO GOOD COULD

SO   HE   TRADED   HER   TO   OLD   ROMANY   BROWN

NOW THERE'S IRISH
THERE'S ENGLISH
THERE'S PIKEY TRAVELLER GYPPO

THEN   THERE'S   THE   REAL   GYPSIES

NOT THAT WE AREN'T

BUT

YE'LL NOTICE WE'RE WHITE LILY-WHITE
IRISH LOOKIN'
ENGLISH LOOKIN'
LOOKS CAN BE DECEIVIN'
THERE'S SOME CLANS SOME TRIBES SOME FAMILIES
GOT THAT TRUE OLD ROMANI WAYS AN' LOOK ABOUT THEM

INCLUDIN'   THAT   DARKER   SKIN

THE OLD BLOOD

THE   ROMANI

THE ROMA

THE   ROM

I'M TALKIN' ABOUT GYPP

E G Y P T

THEY CALL IT GYPP SAYS IT ALL DESCENDS FROM EGYPT
THE ANCIENT WAYS
THE FORTUNE TELLERS
THE HEALERS
THE CASTIN' OF SPELLS

T H E   K N O W L E D G E   O F   T H E   S T A R S

SOOTHSAYIN'
THAT OLD ROMANY BROWN HIM AN' HIS

T H A T ' S   E G Y P T

but it's a misnomer ...

IT'S WHAT WE TOLD THE CHRISTIANS IN THE MIDDLE AGES
THE WHITE MAN
THE WESTERN MAN
THE EUROPEANS

T H E   G A D J E

IT IMPRESSED THEM
CAUGHT THEIR IMAGINATION
APPEALED TO THEIR SENSE OF HISTORY
OLD TESTAMENT
GAVE US SAFE PASSAGE

R E A L L Y   W E ' S   F R O M   I N D I A

ALL GYPSYIES ARE FROM INDIA
OUR FLAG'S GOT THE WHEEL SAME AS THEIRS
AN' OLD ROMANY BROWN
HIM AN' HIS

I S   F A R   M O R E   G Y P S Y   T H A N   A '   I R I S H   T R A V E L L E R

JOE KEPT HIM CLOSE
HE LOOKED AT THEM WITH THE SIDE-EYE
BUT HE KNEW THAT THEY GOT THE REAL REAL OLD WAYS
AN' KEEPS HIM ON IN CASE HE EVER NEEDS IT

B L A C K   M A G I C K

OLD ROMANY BROWN AN' HIS LADIES
THE WIFE
THE MISTRESSES
THE DAUGHTER
THEY GOT SECRET KNOWLEDGE SPELLS TELLIN' OF THE FUTURE
AN' A KNOWLEDGE OF THE PLANTS

FIX YOU UP A POULTICE
COOK YOU UP A POISON

AN' I ALWAYS SEEN THAT HE HELD OLD ROMANY BROWN

C L O S E

EVER SINCE JOHNNY BOY WHIPPED HIM

I N   C A S E   H E   E V E R   C A M E   B A C K

IN THE 'EGYPTIAN' FASHION A DAUGHTER TRADED FOR A GIRLFRIEND
AN' SOME CASH WHICH IS FUNNY

M O N E Y   C A S H   P A P E R

IT ALL STARTED TRADIN' GOATS LAND DAUGHTERS
AN' HERE WE ARE STILL THE SAME

T H E R E ' S   A   T H I N   V E N E E R   O F   C I V I L I Z A T I O N   O N   T H E   W O R L D

YER WORLD
THE WORLD OF TOWN
YE SEE IT IN THE PUBS
YER ALL FIVE TO TEN DRINKS AWAY AN' FIVE TO TEN INSULTS AWAY FROM BEIN' US

W H E T H E R   Y E   K N O W   I T   O R   N O T

WHETHER YE LIKE IT OR NOT
IT'S THERE IF YE SEE IT
IF YER LOOKIN'

I   S E E   I T

E Y E   S E E

THAT'S WHAT I DO FOR JOE - FOR THE CLAN

I   S E E   A L L   O F   I T   E V E R Y T H I N '   A L L   T H E   A N G L E S

PAID TO SEE
AND WE SEE IT ALL OVER YE
IT'S HOW WE CAN SCAM YE AN' PLAY YE SO WELL
WE KNOW YER PRIMAL URGES
WE LIVE THEM

G O O D   B A D   N E I T H E R

YE JUST HIDE THEM ALL AWAY
AT LEAST FOR THE NINE TO FIVE
YE LOOK AT ME LIKE A SAVAGE

T R A D I N '   O N E   G I R L   F O R   A N O T H E R

LOOK ME IN THE EYE AN' YERSELF IN THE MIRROR
AN' TELL ME THAT HALF THE MARRIAGES YE'VE SEEN
WOULDN'T A' BEEN BETTER OFF
IF THIS ONE WENT WITH THAT ONE
INSTEAD OF THAT ONE BEEN WITH THIS

AN'  VICEY  VERSA ?

YE'S DON'T LIKE IT 'CUZ IT'S BASE AN' LOW
COARSE AN' CRUDE

BUT  IT'S  TRUE

OLD ROMANY BROWN DIDN'T HAVE THE POWER OR THE SIZE OF BIG JOE

BUT  HE  HAD  THAT  WICKEDNESS

HE GOT HER SMACKED OUT ON HEROIN GOT HER ON THE JUNK

H   E   R   O   I   N

THAT HEROIN KEPT HER CALM
THEN A ZOMBIE
THEN A SLAVE

then he'd just whore her out for money

S H E ' D   W H O R E   H E R S E L F   O U T   F O R   S M A C K

R O M A N Y  B R O W N  H A D  T O  B U Y  H E R  B A C K  F R O M  T I M E  T O  T I M E

THEY GOT THEIR OWN LANGUAGE
OWN DIALECT
THEIR GAMMON'S DIFF'RENT FROM OURS
OWN CODE
OWN MORALS
SLIT YER THROAT IN THE NIGHT NEVER SEE IT COMIN'

I F  I  C A N ' T  S E E  T H E  M O V E S  T H E  M O T I V E S  I ' M  W A R Y

HE THEY THEM
THEY KEEP ALL SEPARATE MOST OF THE TIME

T H E Y   C A L L E D   H I S   D A U G H T E R   T H E   B L A C K   M A R I A

IT'S A DOUBLE MEANIN'
A PLAY ON THE BLACK MADONNA

P A G A N   M A R Y

AN' IT'S SLANG FOR A PADDY WAGON

T H E   B L A C K   M A R I A

IT WAS A TELL

DARK   GODDESS   A   BLACK   WAGON

THAT TRAPS YE

TAKES   YE   AWAY

THERE'S POWERS IN WORDS
IN NAMES
THERE'S A FORM OF MAGIC SOMEHOW IN THOSE DOUBLE MEANIN'S

JOE   WAS   SMITTEN   WITH   HER

BUT I COULD SEE IT
THEY WERE LININ' HIM UP

THEY'RE   COMIN'   FOR   YER   CROWN

HE'S SAID

        NO FULL-BLOODED TRAVELLER
        EVER BEAT HIM IN AN ACTUAL REAL PROPER BARE-KNUCKLE

WHICH WAS TECHNICALLY TRUE
SO THE CROWN IS HIS

EXCEPT   THE   ROM   DON'T   FIGHT   LIKE   US

THEY'VE   ESOTERIC   WAYS

THEY DON'T STAND THERE RIGHT BEFORE YE
BARE HANDED MAN TO MAN
THEY'RE SUBTLE AN' INDIRECT

IT'S   KEPT   THEM   ALIVE   FOR   THOUSANDS   OF   YEARS

NOW WHEN YER BLINDED BY THE LOVE
THE LUST
YER OWN INFATUATION
WITH THE DAUGHTER OF YER SECRET WEAPON

WHO   PROTECTS   YE   FROM   THEM ?

ROMANY BROWN IS THE PUPPET MASTER
THAT DAUGHTER OF HIS IS A FOUL SORCERESS

BEAUTIFUL   DEADLY   HEMLOCK   A   POISON   FLOWER

BLACK   MAGICK

GOT HER CHARMS AN' SIGHTS AN' SPELLS ON JOE
THEY'LL EITHER SET HIM UP SO JOHNNY BOY TAKES HIM DOWN EASY
OR JUST LAY IN WAIT FOR JOHNNY BOY TO DO THE HEAVY LIFTIN'

WHATEVER THEY ARE SHOWIN' OUTWARDLY
THEY'LL MAKE THEIR MOVES IN SECRET

I N   T H E   D A R K N E S S
AS TRAVELLER AN' GYPP AS WE ARE - THAT ROMANY AN' HIS TRIBE ARE THE DARKNESS

N O T H I N '   I S   A S   I T   S E E M S
THEY MAKE BOTH TRAVELLER AN' IRISH ALIKE WHISPER AN' CHECK THEIR POCKETS

W A T C H   Y E R   B A C K
ALWAYS AN ANGLE

D O U B L E C R O S S A D O U B L E C R O S S T H E N C R O S S I T B A C K A G A I N

AN' JUST LIKE LOA WAS DRUGGED
HOOKED ON THE JUNK
JOE WAS HOOKED ON THE LOVE
HIS LUST
HIS LONGIN'

I   S H O U L D   H A V E   L E F T   T H E N

i should have left

Settled

It's no good Joe
It's foine
It's not fine
Enough – leave it
Listen to me – I'm yer adviser

L E A V E   I T   I   S A Y S

SAYS IT ANYWAY

She's wild Joe
That's exactly why she needs to be settled!

T H I S   I S   N O T   A B O U T   H E R   I T ' S   A B O U T   W H A T   Y E   W A N T

AN' YE WANT HER
IT'S PLAIN AS THE NOSE ON YER FACE
YE GET FIXATED OBSESSED BLINDED BY LOVE
WE SEEN IT ALL BEFORE
THEY ALWAYS SAY THAT LOVE IS BLIND
YER BLINDED BY YER INFATUATIONS

S O   B L I N D   Y E   C A N ' T   S E E   W H A T ' S   C O M I N '

She's not a bad girl!
She's not one of us

N O T   R E A L L Y

They're different – ye know that
That's me point she needs settlin'

A N '   I ' M   T H E   M A N   T O   S E T T L E   H E R

SHE'LL GET
SHE WILL

G R A N T E D   O V E R   T O I M E   S H E ' L L   L E A R N   T O   L O V E   M E

AN' BE – EM THE CLIMATE
WHAT'S THE TERM – CUSTOMIZED?
WHAT'S THE TERM I'M LOOKIN' FER?

C L I M A T A T E D ?

Acclimated?
Aye, that's the one – she'll become accustomated like ye just said
I don't see it Joe
She'll accept it

T H A T ' S   O U R   W A Y   T H A T ' S   H E R   F A T E   A N '   M O I N E

SHE'S THE FINEST LASS FROM THE ROMANI SIDE

T H E   K I N G   N E E D S   A   N E W   Q U E E N

A N '   T H A T   I S   T H A T   A N '   T H A T ' S   I T   F O R E V E R

BESIDES THEIR TRIBE IS FAR MORE 'CUSTOMED TO THESE ARRANGEMENTS THAN EVEN WE'S ARE
Y'KNOW THAT DONCHA?
TO BE PERFECTLY FRANK
I CAN'T BE ARSED - SICK OF FOOKIN' TALKIN' ABOUT IT

Y E ' S   K N O W   S O   M U C H   T H E N   T E L L   M E

T E L L   M E

*if ever joe goes from loud to quiet — he's almost nearly ready to fight ...*
*an' he just got quiet*

WHO RUNS THIS?

*for all his shite ...*
*it's easy to forget he's a very dangerous man*

I SAID FOOKIN' TELL ME

I thought ye was bein' rhetorical
I was bein' fookin' serious
Right
Right what?
What was the question?

I SAID WHO FOOKIN' RUNS THIS?

You Joe
An' who's the leader of this clan?
You Joe
An' who just said how it's gonna be?
You Joe

T H E N   W H A T ' S   T H E   F O O K I N '   P R O B L E M   ?

*someone has to ...*

T H E   P R O B L E M   I S   S H E ' L L   N E V E R   B E   S E T T L E D

SHE'S TOO FREE
SHE'S GOT THE WANDERLUST
SHE NEEDS TO MOVE
SHE CAN'T BE CAGED
SHE CAN'T BE TAMED
SHE WON'T HAVE IT
SHE WON'T STAND IT

I T ' L L   N E V E R   W O R K   N O T   I N   A   M I L L I O N   Y E A R S

IT'LL DRIVE HER MAD
IT'LL DRIVE YE MAD

IT'S ME JOB TO TELL YE THESE THINGS

YE'LL TRY AN' FAIL
AN' IT'S GONNA BRING
YE
HER
US

THE CLAN

NOTHIN' BUT MISERY AN' PAIN

THEIR KIND CAN'T BE TRUSTED JOSEPH
THIS SITUATION CAN'T BE TRUSTED
THEY'LL MOVE AGAINST YE

SHE'S A WITCH

BLACK MAGICK

are ye really gonna make me say it?

SAY HER NAME ?

HAVE YE LEARNED NOTHIN' FROM THAT SUMMER?

YER PREVIOUS FECKIN' MARRIAGE ?

JOE STARES THE STARE OF WANT

WANTING

SHE WAS HER BEST FRIEND JOE

HER DA FOOKIN' WHORED OUT HER BEST FRIEND

YE DECIDED NEITHER ONE WAS GONNA BE PROMISED TO NO ONE

AN' YE FECKIN' KNOW YE DONE IT

SO IT WAS HANDS OFF AN'
THE TWO GYPPPO PRINCESSES HAD RUN THE OF THIS PLACE
THE RULES NEVER FOOKIN' APPLIED TO THEM

THE TWO TEENY QUEENS

THEY ALWAYS DID JUST AS THEY PLEASED 'CUZ OF YE
THE TWO OF THEM THICK AS THIEVES

THEN YE THINK YER GONNA TAME THEM ?

YE THINK ANOTHER FORCED MARRIAGE IS THE ANSWER?
SHE'S GONNA GET ACCLIMATED TO LOVE YE?

SHE'LL CUT YER THROAT IN THE NIGHT !

FECKIN' POISON YE - IF YER LUCKY

YE ASK ME WHAT'S THE PROBLEM JOSEPH ?

THAT'S THE GODDAMNED FOOKIN' PROBLEM

THE TIME CREEPS PAINFUL

I was bein' fookin' rhetorical

*shite ...*

Right on that last one there rhetorical

*fook sake ...*

I see my mistake then

*either way had to be said ...*

Never ye mind, Joe

*never ye mind*

Because A Debt's Forgotten Doesn't Make It Paid

ON THE LASH LOCKED TALKIN' SHITE

Y'ever think this is wrong?
Wrong how?
The whole thing too easy?
Easy?

TWENTY - ODD NEARLY THIRTY YEARS WE BEEN LOOKIN'

Exactly
Exactly what?
Ye've been waitin' to sort this since he was seventeen
He was eighteen a grown man
Right Joe
A legal man
Right Joe

HE WAS EIGHTEEN

RIGHT JOE EIGHTEEN

Now we seen him an' made contact
I think he's comin'

THAT'S THE PLAN

HE KNOWS HE CAN'T RUN
HE HAS TO FACE ME

But
But nothin'

HE SUCKS STALE PUB AIR THROUGH HIS NOSTRILS

AND SPITS IT IN HIS SPEECH

A MAN KNOWS HE CAN'T RUN FOREVER

AN' HE'S NEARLY OVER FORTY NOW - OLDER EVEN
HE KNOWS IF HE EVER HAS A SHOT AT SORTIN' THIS
WITHOUT BEIN' A FOOKIN' COWARD PUSSY 'TIL HIS LAST DYIN' DAYS
HE'LL HAVE TO PAY
ONE WAY OR THE OTHER
HE PAYS

SWIGS A LAST FOAMY SIP BELGIAN LACE IRISH PINT

THIS IS HIS LAST SHOT

HE DOWNS A SHOT OF THE CHEAPEST WELL WHISKEY

AN' THIS ONE'S MOINE !

BaNg

But if he figures out our man?
So what? He hadn't figured out our plan
If he figures out the kid - he figures out the plan
How so?

GENTLY

*when the auld fella's havin' a drink ye wanna mind yerself ...*

WE HAD A PLAN TO SUCKER HIM
PLAY THE LONG GAME
AN' FISH HIM THROUGH OUR BOY
IF HE FIGURES OUT THE KID - THAT KID AIN'T HOLDIN' UP UNDER PRESSURE

HE'LL  KNOW  THAT  WE  GOT  THE  PRESSURE  ON  HIM

AN'  WE  CAN  FOIND  HIM  ANYWHERE

I'm startin' to think we didn't find him, Joe
What?
He found us

WHOLE  THING'S  BEEN  TOO  EASY  WE  CAN'T  TRUST  IT

YER SAYIN' HE FOUND US?
BY APPEARIN' IN A CROWD
AT A BARE-KNUCKLE MATCH
ON FOOKIN' PAY-PER-VIEW
IN THE FECKIN' AUDIENCE?

HOW  THE  FOOK'S  THAT  HIM  FOINDIN'  US  ?

Dunno, bait I suppose?
He's the bait?
Aye, I suppose he'd be his own bait
He's his own bait fer himself?
Exactly, he showed us where he was - we sent that fookin' kid

GOBSHITE

YER TELLIN' ME
HE'S COMIN' T' GET WHAT HE'S BEEN RUNNIN' FROM?
LIKE I SAID
HE KNOWS HE'S OLD
HE IS NOT COMIN' T' FOIGHT YER MAN FER REAL

PROPER  BARE  -  KNUCKLE

THAT'S MY WORLD AN' HE WANTS NO PART OF IT NEVER

NIL

HE'S LIVIN' LIFE OVER THE SHOULDER HEARIN' THE FOOTSTEPS

W E   F O U N D   H I M   B O Y O   W E   F O U N D   H I M

HE KNOWS THE JIG IS UP
HE'S GONNA ATONE

A N   A T O N E M E N T

HE IS GONNA PAY

F E R   E V E R Y T H I N '   F E R   A L L   O F   I T   F E R   W H A T   H E   D O N E

HE'S GONNA BEG ME FER PEACE
HE'S GONNA BEG ME FER MERCY

A N '   I ' L L   M A K E   H I M   P A Y   U S   M O N E Y

BIG MONEY

A   T R I B U T E

TAX

T H E N   W E   G E T   H I M

*joe's thinkin' he's the one that's owed ...*

He's comin' for revenge
Bollocks!
Why Joe?
Why what?
Tell me why it's bollocks, Joe

B E C A U S E   Y E   C A N N O T   B E   Y E R   O W N   B A I T

If supposedly he's tryin' t'be his own bait - then we bite
Who the fook's gonna reel him in?
Hunh?
Who?
So now yer 'Mister Feckin' Bait Shop' - ye fookin' fishmonger?
Who the hell is gonna reel him in?

I F   H E ' S   H I S   O W N   B A I T ?

WHICH HE AIN'T
BECAUSE
FROM A STRATEGIC POINT OF VIEW YE CANNOT BE YER OWN FOOKIN' BAIT!

E V E R Y O N E   K N O W S   T H A T

What?
But even if he was - he's already in our jaws
What?

What what?
Joseph
What's the look?
Nothin' fine whatever ye say, Joe

AYE AYE YES YES YES YES BOYO

JOE CROWDS HIM

WHAT EVER I FOOKIN' SAY

SNAP SNAP

HE CIRCLES HIS FINGER

AN' I SAY BARKEEP ANOTHER ROUND

PONTIFICATES

We found him
Sure Joe
We got to him
Yes Joe
He's cornered
Right Joe
I think ye now see why I run this clan fer a fookin' reason
Aye Joe
Ye fookin' spanner

BARMAN !

Give this cunt my bill

The Night Before The Night Before

JOE MARCHES FROM THE PUB LIKE A BAD ACTOR

OR LIKE A NON-ACTOR BEING ASKED

CAN YOU ACT LIKE YOU'RE MARCHING OUT OF THAT BAR ?

Do this with me arms?
Yes that's terrible - exactly like that ...

AND ACTION !

That is that
That's what?

THE KID DONE GOOD

BOYO'S ALL SET
HE'S ARROIVED
ALL SETTLED IN AT THE BAR
BEEN BAR-BACKIN' - FETCHIN' THE ICE - CUTTIN' THE LIMES - TAPPIN' THE KEGS

FOOK SAKE I KNOW WHAT A FECKIN' BAR-BACK DOES

HE'S MADE CONTACT - CAN'T TALK NOW HE'S GOT NEWS HE SAYS - CALLIN' US BACK

BIG NEWS I FOOKIN' TOLD YA I FOOKIN' TOLD YA

I've got a bad feelin'
About the foight?
Aye

THERE AIN'T NEVER GONNA BE NO FOIGHT

*somethin's comin' joe ...*

SOMETHIN' BAD IS COMIN'

The 'Bad Yank'?

*he's laughin' ...*

We have him roight in our plan
What plan?

YER SAYIN' HE'S PLAYIN' US ?

LIKE SOMEHOW HE'S THE CHESS MASTER?
MANIPULATIN' THE PIECES 'ROUND THE SQUARES

'round the squares?

YE'S KNOW WHAT I'M SAYIN'
MOVIN' THE PIECES
I DON'T PLAY CHESS

What if he does?

B  O  L  L  O  C  K  S

HE'D NEED AN ARMY
HEAR ME BOYO?
HE'D NEED A FOOKIN' ARMY
I SAYS

*he's not listenin'...*

H E ' S   O U T G U N N E D   O U T M O V E D

OUTNUMBERED
OUTMANNED

M E   H E A R I N '   F A D E D

UNDER THE SOUND OF ME OWN PULSE IN ME HEAD
JOE'S VOICE FADED TO A TELE WITH THE SOUND TURNED LOW

P O N T I F I C A T I N '   H I S   T H E O R I E S

*he's wrong ...*

THERE'D BE NO FIGHT THIS
THERE'D BE NO FIGHT THAT

T H E R E ' D   B E   N O   F I G H T   B E C A U S E

THERE'D BE NO FIGHT AN'

J O H N N Y   B O Y   W O U L D   C O M E   W I T H   A   P A Y O F F

A GIANT DUFFLE BAG OF MONEY

B E G G I N ' F O R   F O R G I V E N E S S   T H E N   T H E Y   K I L L   H I M   A N Y W A Y

*that man's gonna beg nothin' from no one ...*

ANOTHER ONE ABOUT IF THERE'S A FIGHT
THEY KILL HIM WIN OR LOSE

T H E Y   C A N ' T   S E E   W H A T   I   C A N   S E E

W H A T   E Y E   C A N

I HAVE DREAMS THAT WE'RE ALL DEAD
I CAN'T SEE EXACTLY HOW
AN' HE'S THERE

J   O   H   N   N   Y   B   O   Y

I KEEP COMIN' BACK TO THERE'S SOMETHIN' WE'RE MISSIN'

SOMETHIN' WE DON'T KNOW ABOUT
SOMETHIN' WE MISSED

LIKE HE'S NOT A MORTAL MAN

OR HE'S THE DEVIL HIMSELF
OR HE'S THE FOOKIN' HOUNDS OF HELL
A GHOST
A WRAITH
A SPIRIT
AN' YE CANNOT FIGHT A SPIRIT
HE'S JUST COMIN'
AN' THE CLOSER IT COMES TO THE DAY - IT'S WHAT I CAN'T SEE
I CAN NO LONGER SEE MESELF PROJECTED INTO THE FUTURE
I CAN'T SEE PAST TOMORROW

I BELIEVE THAT WE ARE ALL GONNA DIE

I FEEL IT IN ME BONES
IN ME IMMORTAL SOUL
SUCH AS IT IS
WE ARE ALL GONNA PAY
I DON'T THINK ANYONE CAN STOP IT

BECAUSE WE DESERVE IT

Huh what?
Oi, boyo are ye daft?
How's that?
Ye fookin' listenin' to a word I says?
Huh, sorry Joe sorry
Now go settle up
Settle what? Ye was drinkin' in there without me?
The call
The call?
Collect from the states!

SO YER 'NOT AS DAFT AS I THINK' DAFT FOOKIN' NEPHEW

CALLED US COLLECT FROM CALIFORNIA AT THE PUB?

SO NO ONE'S GONNA' TRACE IT !

CAN'T BE TRACED TO US
THE PUB PART'S MY IDEA

Johnny Boy's gonna sniff him out quick then isn't he?
Fifty-fifty
How's that?
He either does or he doesn't
Nostra-feckin'-damus - aren't we?

COMEDIAN

*more like nostra-fookin'-dumbass ...*

PAY   THE   FOOKIN'   BARMAN

THEY TRUNDLE BACK TOWARDS

RING   RING   RING   RING

BARKEEP APPEARS ON CUE WITH HIS APRON AND HIS RAG

BAR   FLAG   RAG   WAVING   THEM   DOWN

Joseph! Joseph!
What is it then?
Yer man's callin' collect from the states doncha know?

TOLD   YA   THE   KID   WAS   SOUND

JOE ON THE BLOWER

ROIGHT   THEN   BOYO   TELL   ME   THIS   BIG   NEWS   YA   GOT   FER   ME

JOE'S   MOUTH   AGAPE

SLACK JAW
HE SLOWLY BOWS HIS HEAD PROPPED ON THE BAR BY HIS ELBOWS
HIS WRISTS GO LIMP AS IF A PLAYER FOLDING HIS HAND

FOLDING   HIS   CARDS

FANNING   THEM   DOWN

THROWING HIS HAND
LIKE THOSE OLD-TIMEY BURLESQUE DANCERS
WITH THOSE FANS
HE FAN DANCES THE DECK OF THE BAR - DROPPING THE PHONE
LONG FAT EMPTY FINGERS IN SILENCE

OOOOOOOOOOOOOOOOOOOOOOOOOOOOOOOOOOOOOOOOOOOOOOOOOOOOO

DIAL TONE

Joe? Joe? Joe?

N   O   T   H   I   N   G

WHAT IS IT?
YE LOOK LIKE YE SEEN A GHOST

HE   BUOYS   IN   THE   TIME

THERE ARE NO OTHER WORDS FOR IT

he's here

OOOOOOOOOOOOOOOOOOOOOOOOOOOOOOOOOOOOOOOOOOOOOOOOOOOOOOOOOOOOOOOOOOOOOOOOO

The Terms

JOE'S SECOND ALONE

E X H A L E S
e x h a l e s   t h e   w o r d s

AN' SO IT CAME TO PASS
SOUNDS VERY FORMAL VERY DRAMATIC

I  K N O W
eye know

LIKE I KNOW BECAUSE MY EYES KNOW
THAT'S WHAT I DO FOR JOE

I SEE
eye see

SEE THE MOVES BEFORE THEY'RE MADE
SEE THE IDEA FOR THE MOVE BEFORE IT'S FULLY FORMED
I SEEN A LOT IN THIS LIFE AN' I SEE THIS EVERY FIGHT

E V E R Y   F I G H T

AFTER ALL OF IT
ALL THE PLANS
THE PLOTS THE SCHEMES
AFTER ALL THE SHITE'S BEEN TALKED

A L L   Y E ' V E   S E E N   H E R E

W H E N   T H E   F I G H T   I S   F I N A L L Y   O N

every single time without fail ...

THE STRESS
THE TENSION
THE ANGLES
THE ANGLIN'

F U N N Y   H O W   A N G L I N '   A L S O   M E A N S   F I S H I N '

fishin' for any advantage

WHO WHERE WHEN?
HOW MANY?
WHO'S ARMED?
WHO AIN'T?
THE PLACE?
THE FIELD THE CAMP SOME OTHER CAMP?

S O M E   O T H E R   F E C K I N '   F I E L D   L I K E   I T   F O O K I N '   M A T T E R S

SOMETIMES A WAREHOUSE

A B A N D O N E D

ANY FALLS?
JOE'S HEADBUTTS?
THE ODDS?
WHO SETS 'EM? AN' THE POLITICS OF WHY THOSE ODDS ARE THE ODDS


T H E N   T H E   M O N E Y

I T ' S   A L L   A B O U T   T H E   F O O K I N '   M O N E Y

always the money ...

THEN'S THE BETS
WHO'S TAKIN'?
WHO'S HOLDIN'?
SPOTTIN'?
COVERIN'?
PUNTS?
DOLLARS?
POUNDS?


now it's euros ...

W H E N

EVERY BOAST
EVERY THREAT
EVERY BRAG
EVERY PROMISE

WHEN EVERY LINE A' SHITE'S BEEN TALKED AN' SENT ON VIDEO

T H E   C A L L O U T S

WE'RE FAMOUS FOR IT
PRO WRESTLIN'S GOT NOTHIN' ON US


T H E N   A N '   O N L Y   T H E N

START'S THE BITCHIEST QUEENIN' PONCIEST MOST PRECIOUS FECKIN' NIT-PICKIN'

L I K E   Y E   N E V E R   S E E N   A N '   C O U L D N ' T   B E L I E V E   I T   I F   Y E   D I D

THE BACKUP PLACE IF THE GARDAI SHOW?
THE REF
THE 'FAIR PLAY' MAN
THE WRAPS?
THE TAPE?

A N '   N O W   T H I S   H A R D   M A N

A PROPER MAN TOO MIND YE
HARD AS FOOK

SAYS IT ON THE VIDEO

I N S I S T I N ' O N H E ' L L B E N E E D I N ' A F E C K I N ' G U M - S H I E L D

WHO ELSE IS FIGHTIN'?
WHAT'S THE ORDER?

T H E N B A C K T O T H O S E B E T S

THE BETS
THE BETS

M O N E Y

ALWAYS WONDERED WHY THEY NEVER WONDER ABOUT ALL THE BETTIN' ON ALL THESE FAMILIAL THINGS

S I L E N C E

THIS ONE WASN'T POSTURIN'
THIS ONE WAS A BLOOD FEUD

T H I S W A S B L O O D

T H I S W A S W A R

an' it got too real for joe ...

FOR THE FIRST TIME EVER I SEEN HIM
EYE SEEN HIM
EYE SEEN

E Y E K N O W

EYE KNOW NOW
EYE NOW KNOW

i seen that big joe knew he was auld man an' all the shite the lies the hype in the world ...

A I N ' T N E V E R G O N N A S A V E H I M

AN' WHEN
WHEN
HA!
WHEN'S NOW

W H E N I S N O W
now is when ...

E X H A L E S
e x h a l e s t h e w o r d s

AN' SO IT CAME TO PASS
THAT JOHNNY BOY SAID

        I'LL MEET YOUR MAN THE DAY BEFORE
        I'LL MEET WITH YOUR SECOND TO SET THE TERMS
        I DON'T WANT YOUR SHIT

Y O U R   T A L K   T H E   G Y P P O   T H I N G   T H E   A N G L E S

        SEND YOUR FUCKING MAN TO THE FIELD AND WE'LL SORT THE TERMS
        THE NEXT DAY WE FIGHT
        AND WE SETTLE THIS THING

JOE SAID YES
THAT'S ALL HE SAID

A   Q U I E T   G A S P I N G   Y E S

WAS HE AFRAID TO FACE HIM?

Y E S

SOME SAID HE HAD A PLOT TO MAKE A MOVE ON JOHNNY BOY AT THE SETTIN' OF THE TERMS
AN' JOHNNY BOY KNEW OR AT LEAST FIGURED SOMETHIN' ALONG THOSE LINES
OTHERS SAID HE WAS USIN' MY ABSENCE TO PLAN A NUMBER ON HIM
ON THE DAY I WOULD SET THE TERMS

A T   T H E   F I E L D

HIM AN' THE JOE JUNIORS WAS SETTIN' TO DO THAT DIRT - PLANNIN' IT

B E H I N D   M Y   B A C K   E V E N

STILL OTHERS WAS SAYIN'
HE'S GONNA PLAN TO CALL THE GARDAI ON HIS OWN FIGHT
GET HIMSELF ARRESTED
EVEN DO A STINT IN JAIL TO KEEP HIMSELF SAFE AN' HAVE THAT EXCUSE

P E O P L E   T A L K

AN' GYPPOS TALK MORE THAN PEOPLE

T H E R E   W A S   A   P L A N   I ' D   H A V E   K N O W N

I WOULDA PLANNED IT

E N O U G H   T A L K   L E T ' S   F I G H T

THAT WAS JOHNNY BOY'S WAY
JOE WANTS ROUNDS?

H A V E   I T

JOE WANTS WRAPS?

H A V E   I T

WANT TAPE?
WANT SKIN?

G I V E   H I M   A N Y T H I N '   H E   W A N T S

SO HE CAN'T PULL OUT ON NOT GETTIN' TERMS

H I S   T E R M S

I CAME TO MEET JOHNNY BOY AT THE FIELD

B U T   H E   N E V E R   S H O W E D

JOE HIT ME ON THE BURNER TO GET THE STORY

     DID HE TAKE THE TERMS?
     'CUZ IF HE DIDN'T

E T   C E T E R A   E T   C E T E R A   E T   C E T E R A   A N '   S O   F O R T H

an' i'm standin' alone in a feckin' field y'know

     WE'RE WORKIN' IT OUT I SAYS
     SAYS I'LL CALL HIM BACK
     BYE BYE BYE

i fold up the burner

JUST THEN A KID ON A BIKE COMES UP IN A FOOKIN' HALLOWEEN COSTUME OF SOME SORT

C A P E   A N '   A   M A S K

H E Y   M I S T E R   Y O U   T H E   S E C O N D ?

FOOK SAKE THE FOOK IS THIS?

A N   A M E R I C A N   S A Y S   I ' M   T O   G I V E   Y A   T H I S   B U R N E R

HE HOLDS IT OUT TO ME

G O   O N   T H E N   M I S T E R   T A K E   I T

I BLANKED
IT GAVE ME A QUARE FEELIN'
THAT FEELIN' YE'VE BEEN OUTSMARTED
THAT FEELIN' THAT YE'VE LOST
THAT FEELIN' THAT YE ARE LOST
THE FEELIN' OF FEAR FEELIN' OF FATE
WHEN FATE FINALLY FINDS YOU

H E Y   M I S T E R   D O N ' T   Y O U   W A N T   I T ?

T I M E

HE PAID ME TO GIVE IT TO YA

HE  SAID  IT'S  TERRIBLY  IMPORTANT

Aye aye yeah yeah sure son
Ok, bye now mister
Say who are ye under there?

HE TURNED HIS MASKED FACE SLOWLY BACK TO ME AS HE RODE AWAY

I'M  THE  HARBINGER  OF  FUCKING  SORROWS  AREN'T  I ?

CHING CHING CHING CHING
BIKE  BELL  BIKE  BELL

AN'  HE  DISAPPEARED

IT UNSETTLED ME
AN OMEN
A VISION
ALL THE GYPP IN ME TURNED SOUR
BLOOD TURNED COLD

S U P E R S T I T I O N

CURSES AN' MAGICK IS REALER THAN YE THINK
AN' THAT WAS SOME WITCHY SHIT RIGHT THERE

I  JUST  STOOD  THERE  UNTIL  THE  MIST  TOOK  THE  KID

SAME AS IT DELIVERED HIM

THAT  CREEPY  BIKE  BELL  RINGIN'  IN  THE  FOG

F R O Z E   M E

FROZEN

CHING CHING CHING CHING
RING  RING  RING  RING

THE BIKE BELL RINGIN' SOMEHOW BECAME THE PHONE RINGIN'
RINGIN' IN A DOUR DOOMFUL WAY – THE TOLLIN' BELL

F O R   W H O M   T H E   B E L L   T O L L S

HELLO?
AYE
AYE
NO, AYE HE'LL BE THERE
YE'VE GOT ME WORD ON IT

the phone air lay dead an' cold as the chill that ghost kid gave me ...

C O L D E R   E V E N

NOW WHEN A MAN IS NERVOUS
HE'LL DO SOMETHIN' STUPID
AN' I DID
DON'T KNOW WHY I SAID WHAT I SAID
I SAID SOMETHIN' STUPID

S T U P I D

I MEANT NOTHIN' BY IT

always liked johnny boy ...

I'M STANDIN' THERE ON THAT BURNER IN THE MISTY FIELD AN' ALL THAT TENSION
THE EMPTINESS OF THAT

S   I   L   E   N   C   E

I FILLED THE SPACE
DON'T KNOW WHY
COULDN'T TAKE IT I SUPPOSE
AN' SAID

         SO HOW HAVE YE BEEN JOHNNY?

THEN A SCARIER SILENCE

T E R R I F Y I N G

i got no words now for ye - there's just ...

I COULD HEAR AN' FEEL THE HEAT OF BREATH LIKE HE'S BEHIND ME
RIGHT THERE IN THAT FIELD
JUST THE DEADEST AIR MEANT FOR ME

I F   H E   D O E S N ' T   S H O W   I   W I L L   F U C K I N G   K I L L   Y O U

FOLDED THE BURNER
EYES TO THE GROUND
POCKETED IT

A N '   O F   C O U R S E   A S   W E   N O W   K N O W

E X H A L E S
e x h a l e s   t h e   w o r d s

joe never showed ...

The Fight

THE  FIGHT  WAS  SET  FOR  THE  CAMP  AT  DAWN

JOHNNY BOY WAS THERE

S O L O

LEAN THIN EYES ON QUIET FIRE
CARVED OUTTA WOOD
READY
READY TO FOOKIN' FIGHT
READY TO KILL
READY FOR

A  N  Y  T  H  I  N  '

I NEVER SEEN A MAN MORE READY FOR ANYTHIN'
ANYWHERE ANYTIME EVER
THAT'S A READY MAN
READY AN' RELAXED
THAT'S A CAPABLE MAN

C A P A B L E   O F   A N Y T H I N '   I   T H O U G H T

HE SORTA STAYED AROUND SOME OF THE OLD CAMP FRIENDS HE HAD
THEY ALL LOVED LOA
AN' THERE'S MORE N' A FAIR SHARE OF OUR CLAN THAT'S READY IN THEIR OWN WAY
TO SEE SOME JUSTICE

T H E Y   L A M E N T E D   H E R   A L L   M O R N I N G

they lamented her all mourning

HE'S NURSIN' THIS GIGANTIC CUPPA STARBUCKS
THINK OF THAT
EVEN HERE THE CARAVANS AREN'T THAT FAR AWAY FROM TOWN
FECKIN' STARBUCKS
IT'S ALL COUNCIL PLOTS NOW
MOST OF US ONLY TRAVEL IN THE SUMMERS PART-TIME
THEY GOT REALITY SHOW'S ON TRAVELLERS NOW

N O W   H E ' S   S T A N D I N '   T H E R E

THOUSAND-YARD STARE

G I A N T   P A P E R   C U P P A
in his hand

T H A T   R I G H T   H A N D

I REALISED I WASN'T STARIN' AT THE CUP
I WAS STARIN' AT HIS HAND

S C R A P E D   T H E   F O O K '   U P

B L O O D Y   S C R A T C H E S

DIRT UNDER THE NAILS
WRAPPED IN GAUZE
TAPED UP HASTILY QUICK-LIKE

N O T   T A P E D   F O R   A   F I G H T

Ye injured there son?
Practice

HE SPIT THE WORD WITHOUT LOOKIN' AT ME EVEN

T H E N   T H E   S U N   H I T   N O O N

Where is he?

fook i haven't seen joe yet this mornin'
haven't heard his big loud boomin' fookin' voice
the man never shuts up

H E   N E V E R   S H U T S   U P

shite fook' shite - nah never there's no way ...

I RAN TO JOE'S CARAVAN
HIS COMPOUND
HE'S GOT LIKE FOUR CARAVANS

AN' THERE'S NO ONE

NO JOE NO BOYS
NO ONE
NO SIGN OF NOTHIN' WRONG NEITHER
NO SIGNS OF PACKED BAGS
NO STRUGGLE

N O T H I N ' S   L E F T   O N
no one left in a hurry

I CHECKED AROUND AN' BEIN' HIS SECOND I KNOW HE'S GOT A STASH AN' I KNOW WHERE IT'S KEPT
NOTHIN' AMISS
PLASTIC BAG OF CASH
GOLD COINS
PAPERS OF SOME SORT

A N '   T H E   G U N

I KNOW I SHOULDN'T HAVE
BUT IF JOE DOESN'T SHOW

I   P O C K E T E D   T H E   R E V O L V E R

DOUBLE-TIMED IT BACK TO JOHNNY BOY

TRYIN' TO WALK SLOWER
AN' LOOK CALMER THAN I WAS
I HELD THE GUN IN ME POCKET

Q U I E T L Y   C O C K E D   I T

He's not here

HE WINKS

*did he just fookin' wink?*

I'll get him on the mobile

I TOOK OUT ME BURNER

RING RING RING RING

NO JOE
NO ANSWER
NO VOICEMAIL
NO NOTHIN'

H E ' S   S I P P I N '   T H A T   C U P

HE'S GOT A CUT ON THE BRIDGE OF HIS NOSE?

H E ' S   B E E N   I N   A   F I G H T

NOW I GOT THE HEATER IN THE POCKET
DIALIN' LEFTY
AN' I CAN SEE HE SEES THIS
AN' I CAN SEE HE DOESN'T CARE

    I SAID DAWN
    HE SAYS
    WE AGREED
    I SAYS
    LET'S GIVE HIM 'TIL SUNDOWN

H E   S M I L E S   A N '   S I P S   T H A T   P A P E R   C U P

Then ye gonna kill me son?

HE KINDA LAUGH-SIP-SNORT-SPITS HIS COFFEE
AS IF IT'S THE FUNNIEST THING HE'S EVER HEARD
THEN I FOR BETTER OR WORSE

an' believe you me - it was for the worse ...

M A D E   M E   F O O K I N '   M O V E

I   A T T E M P T   T O   P U L L   T H E   G U N   O U T

BUT I HAD COCKED IT
AN' I FUMBLED IT LIKE A COMEDY NUMBER
I HAD ME WELL-WORN OLD LEATHER
THE OLD BAGGY POCKET LINER'S TORN
AN' I'M LIKE FOOKIN' WITH THIS TORN FECKIN' POCKET LINER

B U T

THE HAMMER'S BACK
SO'S I HAVE TO BE GENTLE AS I TRY TO MAKE ME FINAL STAND
MIND YOU THIS IS ME OSTENSIBLY FIGHTIN' FOR ME OWN LIFE HERE
THE MENTAL FOOKIN' EEJIT THAT APPARENTLY I AM

A N '   I T   A L L   W E N T   A R S E W A Y S

HE ACTS IT OUT

T H I S   I S   M E

stumblin' fumblin' cunt that i am ...

A N '   H E ' S   J U S T   S T A N D I N '   T H E R E

NOT CHUFFED
NOT SCARED
NOT NOTHIN'

B E M U S E D

AN' I SWEAR TO GOD
SWEAR TO GOD HE SAYS

     GOOD YOU GOT THE GUN

S A Y S   N O T   A S K S

I RAISED THE BURNER IN ME LEFT
IT'S LIKE I'M WATCHIN' MESELF ON TELE
OUT OF BODY EXPERIENCE - WHAT HAVE YE
AN' I OFFER UP THE PHONE AS IF IT'S A SHIELD OR A TALISMAN'S GONNA SOMEHOW PROTECT ME

i kinda ducked an' squinted me eyes ...

FINALLY CLEAR THE GUN OUT ME POCKET
HAD TO CAREFULLY UN-COCK IT AN' THE HAMMER GRABBED THE LINER
TEARIN' THE LININ' AN' IT'S GOT FABRIC STUCK ON THE HAMMER
AN' I SEE THAT THE LINER IS LIKE A LITTLE FLAG

W H I T E   F L A G   O F   S U R R E N D E R

I DROPPED THE PHONE WHICH STARTLED ME AN' I FLINCHED
SO THERE I AM INADVERTENTLY WAVIN' THIS WHITE FLAG
AS I'M BRINGIN' ME HANDS TOGETHER TO FIRE IT
AN' HE'S JUST FECKIN' LOOKIN' AT ME

THEN  I  STARTED  BABBLIN'

A LITANY ON JOE AN' ALL THE TERRIBLE THINGS HE'D DONE
ALL HIS SINS
STARTED PLEADIN'
HOW'S YE CAN'T MURDER ME FOR JOE BEIN' A HORRIBLE PERSON AN' A RAPIST

AGAIN  A  MAN  IS  NERVOUS

IT JUST WENT ON AN' ON FOR WHAT SEEMED LIKE FOREVER
AT SOME POINT I REALIZED THAT I'VE GOT THE GUN
AN' HE'S GOT A COFFEE
WHICH TO BE PERFECTLY HONEST MADE THE WHOLE THING FEEL EVEN MORE PATHETIC

I  STARTED  TO  WEEP

NOT PROUD OF IT
BUT THAT'S WHAT HAPPENED
I CLOSED ME EYES
CRYIN' LIKE A BABY

PULLED  THE  TRIGGER

cLiCk

THE  ENTIRETY  OF  ME  WORLD  STOPPED

the sound of that click was louder than any gunshot i thought i was prepared for

I OPENED ONE EYE

cLiCk

SHITE

cLiCk

NOW  I  AM  PROPER  FUCKED

HOW MANY CLICKS THAT WAS THAT?
THREE CLICKS?
THREE MORE?
BY THIS POINT THE ENTIRE CLAN'S JUST LOOKIN' AT ME
ACUTELY AWARE OF THE EXTENT TO WHICH I AM FUCKED

I  LET  OUT  A  PRIMAL  WAIL

THAT  WAS  PARTICULARLY  LESS  THAN  MASCULINE

AGAIN NOT PROUD
AN' I'M GONNA DO IT FOR YE NOW FOR THE SAKE OF CLARITY
AN' IN THE NAME HISTORICAL ACCURACY
THE SOUND OF ME IMMORTAL SOUL WHEN IT'S UP AGAINST IT

ME ANCIENT CELTIC BATTLE CRY

SOUNDS LIKE THIS

## NAAAAIIIIIIIIIIIIIIEEEEEEEEUHHHHHHHHHH

THE 'UNIQUE' TONE OF MY WAIL DEVOLVED INTO MORE SOBBIN' N' CRYIN'
AS I ATTEMPTED TO COUNT THE REMAININ' CLICKS

FOUR

cLiCk

FIVE

cLiCk

WHEREUPON I TURNED THE BY NOW QUITE OBVIOUSLY EMPTY GUN

TO  ME  OWN  TEMPLE

BECAUSE AT THAT POINT MAYBE A LUCKY BULLET
WOULD JUST MAGICALLY APPEAR AN' DELIVER ME FROM THIS FARCE

*like the coward that i am ...*

I  UGLY  CRIED  AS  I  MOUTHED  THE  WORD

SIX

cLiCk

THEN  I  JUST  SAT  DOWN  FOR  A  DRY-CRY

SOBBIN' BUT OUT OF TEARS
LIKE A DRY-HEAVE
BUT FOR THE EYES AN' THE SOUL

> THE GUN'S EMPTY
> HE SAYS
> GOOD GOOD KUSHTI
> I SAYS

was the best i could manage

HE'S  SMILIN'  AT  THE  WHOLE  THING

> I'M NOT GOING TO KILL YOU
> OH OK THANK YOU

I  LITERALLY  SAID  THANK  YOU

actually wouldn't have minded if he did

HE TALKED TO ROMANY BROWN SOME
SUSSIN' THINGS SORTIN' THINGS
I ASSUME
WHAT THE FOOK WOULD I KNOW?

I    J U S T    S A T    T H E R E

SOMEONE GAVE ME WATER
SOMEONE MADE ME TEA

        BUG A GUSHACH WEED?
        AR MUNYA DIL?
        AR MUNYA HU?

I    J U S T    S T A Y E D    T H E R E    W A T C H I N '    H I M

WATCHIN' HIM TALK
WATCHIN' HIM WATCHIN' ME WATCHIN' HIM
JUST KEPT LOOKIN' AT THOSE HANDS THEN HIS FACE

T H E    D I R T    T H E    N A I L S    T H E

T R U T H

*hit me ...*

H E    K I L L E D    J O E

HE KILLED JOE AN' HIS BOYS
HE DONE IT ALREADY

H O W ?

WHEN?

*when i was at the field ...*

W A I T I N '    F O R    T H E    G H O S T    K I D

I ABSENTLY RUBBED ME EYES AN' SMELLED THE GUN

F L I N T    A N '    P O W D E R

IT WOKE ME UP

        THAT GUN'S EMPTY

*he knew ...*

JOE AN' HIS TWO BOYS
TWO SLUGS A PIECE
I RECKON
THREE TIMES TWO MAKES SIX
THAT'S HOW HE KNEW

H E   E M P T I E D   I T

HE INTENDED ME TO FIND IT
GET ME PRINTS ALL OVER IT
ALL OVER THE GUN THAT KILLED JOE
I'M HOLDIN' IT
NOW NO ONE'LL EVER CALL THE GARDAI

C   H   E   C   K   M   A   T   E

*we was playin' checkers ...*

I SAT UNTIL THE SUN WENT

T H E   S K Y   B L E D   S T R E A K S   O R A N G E   P U R P L E

I SAT A LUMP OF SCARLET

    ROMANY'S GOT SOME STUFF TO TELL YOU AT YOUR CARAVAN
    HE SAID - I THINK
    YOU'LL GET THE CLAN TOGETHER AT THE FIRE AND TELL THEM HOW THINGS ARE GONNA BE
    SOMETHIN' LIKE THAT

HE'D FINISHED BY THE TIME I KNEW HE WAS EVEN TALKIN' TO ME
I WASN'T HEARIN' RIGHT

    HEY
    HE SAYS
    YOU UNDERSTAND?
    YES SON - YES SIR - I MEAN - JOHNNY

T H E   L O O K   H E   S H O T   M E   F O R   T A L K I N '   E X T R A

    I'M SORRY
    DO YOU UNDERSTAND?

I NODDED
I COULD ONLY HEAR MUFFLED TONES AN' THE THROBBIN' OF ME PULSE IN ME OWN HEAD
I GOT LOST IN ME OWN THOUGHTS
JUST ONE THOUGHT REALLY

    *our way is dyin'   our way is dyin'   our way is dyin'   our way is dyin'*

    D O   Y O U   F U C K I N G   U N D E R S T A N D   M E ?

    yes

tHE LAST gYppo kiNg

THE  SUN  WENT  FIRE  LIT

JOHNNY BOY STOOD FLANKED BY ME AN' OLD ROMANY BROWN
WE BACKED HIM AS THE WINNER BY WAY OF

F O R F E I T

JOE 'RAN AWAY' WE SAID

A B A N D O N E D   T H E   C L A N

HIS STANDIN' HIS POSITION AS LEADER
HIS TITLE
NOW JOHNNY BOY IS THE

G Y P S Y   K I N G

HE EVEN WENT SO FAR AS TO SAY HE'D TAKE ON ANY-AN'-ALL COMERS
FOR SHOW
NO ONE DARED
HE EXPLAINED HOW HE ONLY WANTED JUSTICE

T H I S   W E   K N E W

HE SAID HE WAS LEAVIN' AN' NEVER COMIN' BACK

T H I S   W E   K N E W   A S   W E L L

HE LEFT IT TO US TO CHOOSE THE NEW LEADER

T H E N   H E   W H I S P E R E D   S O M E T H I N'   T O   R O M A N Y   B R O W N

H E   G A V E   H I M   S O M E   E N V E L O P E S

some letters ...

HE LOOKED ME DEAD IN THE EYES WHEN HE DONE IT

I   G O T   L O S T   T H I N K I N'   W H A T' S   I N   T H O S E   E N V E L O P E S ?

I COULDN'T HOLD HIS GAZE
LOOKED AWAY FOR LESS THAN A SECOND
LESS THAN THE TIME TO BLINK
LOOKED BACK AN' HE WAS GONE
LIKE THE GHOST KID FROM THE FIELD
LIKE JOE AN' HIS BOYS

D   I   S   A   P   P   E   A   R   E   D

ROMANY GOT BEHIND ME FOR THE VOTE
EVEN WITH ALL THE CRYIN' I DONE

T H E Y   W E N T   F O R   M E

NO ONE KNEW EXACTLY HOW HE DID WHAT HE DID

if he did ...

L E T ' S   F A C E   I T   H E   D I D

THEN VERY SOON AFTER - JUST A COUPLE DAYS REALLY
PEOPLE JUST

S T O P P E D

STOPPED ASKIN'
STOPPED CARIN'
STOPPED TRYIN' TO FIGURE IT OUT

B E C A U S E   A S   S H O C K I N '   A S   I T   W A S

THE BAD YANK COME BACK OVER AN' JUST

D I S A P P E A R I N '   J O E

MAYBE HE RAN?
MAYBE I'D HAVE RAN?
WHO KNOWS?
BUT WITH HIM BEIN' SUCH AN OPPRESSIVE CUNT

C U N T

A RIGHT FOOKIN' CUNT
NO GOOD NEVER WAS
NEVER ANY GOOD TO ANYONE BUT HIMSELF
AN' EVERYONE WOULD TELL YE THE SAME

N O W   H E ' S   G O N E

SOMEONE SAID ROMANY TOLD JOHNNY BOY WHERE LOA WAS BURIED
AN' HE DUG UP HER BONES WITH HIS BARE HANDS
DUG HER UP OUT OF LOVE
HER RED HAIR - HER BONES - AN' HE BURNED THEM IN A FIRE AT THE SITE OF HER OLD CAMP
HER SPECIAL PLACE
AN' THOSE ENVELOPES WAS MONEY THANKIN' HIM FOR IT

O T H E R S   S A Y S   I T ' S   A   M A P   T O   W H E R E   J O E   W A S   B U R I E D

TRUST ME WHEN I SAY IT WAS LETTERS

B U T   T H A T ' S   A N O T H E R   S T O R Y

THE GARDAI NEVER CAME - IF THEY DID WE'D NEVER HAVE TALKED

J O E   W A S   G O N E

JOHNNY DIDN'T WANT IT
NOR ROMANY

AN' THOUGH I NEVER WANTED IT
NEVER ASKED FOR IT
AN' CERTAINLY NEVER FOUGHT FOR IT

T H A T ' S   H O W   I   B E C A M E

THE LAST GYPPO KING

e p i l o g u e

Landed Gentry

THEY  SAID  HE  MADE  IT  BIG  IN  REAL  ESTATE

SAID IT WAS THE FURTHEST FROM BEIN' A TRAVELLER
SOME SAID HE TOOK OVER FOR HIS DA
AN' REALLY SHOWED THEM RACKET BOYS WHAT A GANGSTER IS

PROPER  FOOKIN'  GANGSTER

THAT HE WAS CONNECTED

SAID  YE'D  NEED  THAT  TO  DISAPPEAR  JOE  LIKE  THAT

IRISH MOB
IRA
THE MAFIA
WHITEY BULGER

THE  KIND  OF  PEOPLE  HIS  DA  RAN  WITH

OTHERS SAID THIS
OTHERS SAID THAT
AS THE NIGHT WENT AN' THE BOOZE FLOWED
SO DID ALL THE

THEORIES

JOE PAID OFF JOHNNY BOY
JOE'S WORKIN' WITH THE GARDAI AN' ALWAYS HAD BEEN

THEN  THERE'S  THE  EXCESSIVELY  INTRICATE

BLACK  MAGICK  MOTORBIKE  THEORY

THE BLACK MARIA WAS SECRETLY IN LOVE WITH
AN' IN LEAGUE WITH JOHNNY BOY - EVER SINCE SHE RAN OFF TO AVOID MARRYIN' JOE

ALWAYS  KEEPIN'  HER  EAR  TO  THE  GROUND  THEY  SAID

KEPT HER ONE EYE ON US THROUGH HER PEOPLE
AN' KEPT HER OTHER ON JOHNNY BOY THROUGH HER MAGICK

HER  SPELLS

IT GOES THAT SHE LET HIM KNOW ABOUT LOA

HER  SUICIDE

HELPED HIM PLOT THE DETAILS THE WHEN AN' WHERE
HELPED TO LURE THEM MAYBE EVEN USED HERSELF AS BAIT

WHICH  IT'S  BEEN  SAID  YE  CAN  NOT  EVEN  DO

THE MORE THAT BOTTLE EMPTIED
THE MORE ELABORATE IT BECAME

THE KEY MIND YE
WAS JOHNNY BOY LEFT ON A MOTORBIKE

W H I C H   N O   O N E   E V E R   S E E N   M I N D   Y E

NO ONE

BUT PEOPLE SAID THEY HEARD IT AN' THAT SOMEHOW PROVES SOMETHIN'

L I K E   F U L L   C I R C L E

THAT IT WAS MIKEY'S VINCENT BLACK LIGHTNIN'
FROM THE OLD DAYS
JUST LIKE THE SONG

E X A C T   S A M E   B I K E   I N   F A C T

B O L L O C K S

MIKE'S LONG SINCE PASSED AN' ALL HIS BIKES WAS SOLD
THAT BEIN' SAID BY THE END OF THAT BOTTLE I'D CONVINCED MESELF I HEARD A MOTORBIKE

M A Y B E   E V E N   S E E N   I T

THE BLACK MARIA WAITIN' FOR HIM
AN' THEY SAID THEY WENT DEEP INTO HUNGARY OR ROMANIA
AN' BECAME THE KING AN' QUEEN OF THIS OLD-SCHOOL ROMANI TRIBE

T H A T   T H I S   W A S   H E R   P L A N   A L L   A L O N G

SHE HATED HER FATHER FOR WHAT HE DONE TO HER FRIEND
SHE HATED JOE AN' ALL THE TINKER MEN
AN' THIS WAS HER REVENGE

S H E   C A S T   A   S P E L L   U S E D   H I M   A S   A   W E A P O N

GOBSHITE

tinkers on the lash ...

OLD ROMANY BROWN AN' HIS SET OFF
THEY'D BEEN SETTLED TOO LONG AN' THEIR DEAL WITH JOE WAS OVER
AN' OF COURSE THEY'S ALL SAID THEY WAS GOIN' TO JOIN JOHNNY BOY AN' THE BLACK MARIA

I N   T H E   M O R N I N '   M E   H A N G O V E R   D I S M I S S E D   I T

FORGOT IT EVEN

F I R S T   D A Y   I N   P O W E R   I ' M   S H A T T E R E D

*pissed wrecked scuttered fucked ...*

I N   F O O K I N '   B I T S

THAT NEXT NIGHT THE WORD

ROMANY   BROWN   AN'   HIS   FAMILY   NEVER   MADE   IT

WHAT WE GATHER IS THEY TRAVELED OVERNIGHT AN' PEACEFULLY THAT DAY

THEN   TWILIGHT   CAME

THEY PULLED ASIDE TO CAMP
AS THE SUN SET IT BROUGHT A WEIRD EERIE LIGHT
ON THE TRAIL
IN THE WOODS

IN   THE   GLOAMING

THEY   WERE   RIPPED   APART   BY   GUNFIRE

ALL THEIR CARAVANS WERE BURNED

THAT   PART   RIGHT   THERE
THAT WAS THE TELL

THE OLD WAY
A TRAVELLER DIES YE'D BURN HIS WAGON AN' ALL HIS POSSESSIONS

THAT   WAS   THE   MESSAGE

GOT   ME   THINKIN'   OF   THOSE   LETTERS
THAT'S WHEN I KNEW

THOSE   ENVELOPES

I REMEMBER THINKIN' IT'S GOTTA BE A PAYOFF

MONEY

TO ROMANY
FOR HELPIN' SET UP JOE
AN' THAT JOHNNY BOY DIDN'T KNOW ABOUT HIM AN' LOA

COULDN'T   KNOW   'CUZ   YE'D   NEVER   PAY   ANYONE   WHO

NEVER

NOT HIM
NOT EVER

NOT   IN   A   MILLION   YEARS

THEN IT HIT ME WHATEVER'S IN THOSE ENVELOPES
NOT MONEY

M A Y B E   L E T T E R S

BURNED AWAY FOREVER
JUST LIKE HIS DEAD BODY
AN' EVERYTHIN' HE LOVED AN' OWNED AN' EVER CARED ABOUT

W O U L D   I T   C O M E   T O   M E   T H A T   W A Y   ?

if so when?

ALWAYS IN THE BACK OF ME MIND
NEVER REALLY FREE
NEVER AT EASE
NEVER AT PEACE

A L W A Y S   A N '   I N   A L L   W A Y S

W A I T I N '

LIKE SHE DID
LIKE HE DID

like we made them feel ...

this is me fate

An Envelope

RETURN ADDRESS WAS A HOUSING ESTATE                    INTERNATIONAL AIR MAIL STAMP
KILCLARE CRESCENT, JOBSTOWN, TALLAGHT DN 24 IE          THAT WAS DECADES OLD




                    IT HAD HIS MOTHER'S OLD ADDRESS
                    I T S O M E H O W G O T 2 H I M




E N C L O S E D   W A S A L E T T E R W R A P P E D A R O U N D

The First Letter

OPENED IN GAELIC

# A C U S H L A

MY LOVE
MY HEART

# THE PULSE IN MY VEIN

in me

THROUGH ME
PLEASE FORGIVE ME

# FORGIVE ME

forgive me my life trapped here in these ways

# I WAS JUST SIXTEEN

HAVING NO TICKETS NO PASSPORT NO PAPERS OF ANY KIND I COULD CROSS NO BORDERS WITH YOU LEGALLY
YOU WERE THE BRIGHTEST SUMMER OF MY LIFE
AND I THINK I WAS YOURS AS WELL

# IT BREAKS MY HEART YOU AND I STAR-CROSSED LOVERS

romeo & juliet

# MONTAGUE & CAPULET

YOU'LL SEE MY TEARS HITTING THE INK AND SMUDGING THE PAPER
THESE INK-STAINED TEARS WILL DRY ALL FUNNY THE WAY WET PAPER DOES

I LOVE YOU
I LOVED YOU
I LOVE YOU STILL

# MORE THAN ANYTHING MORE THAN ANYONE

I LONGED TO BE WITH YOU BUT MY STORY IS SAD AND TRAGIC
AND NO MATTER HOW I WANTED IT TO BE
WISHED IT TO BE

i fear i was fated to suffer this

# IF ONLY WE WERE BOTH EIGHTEEN

WE MAYBE COULD HAVE RUN AWAY
MAYBE WE COULD HAVE FOUND A WAY

# BUT THAT'S THE PAST AND THE PAST IS GONE

TURNS OUT I WASN'T EVER PREGNANT
NOT AT ALL

SO I'M WRITING TO TELL YOU THAT
AND TO RELIEVE YOU OF ANY STRESS OR WORRY YOU MIGHT HAVE HAD
I WAS JUST A LITTLE LATE IS ALL

just a little late ...

I HOPE YOU GO FORWARD AND FORGET ABOUT ME
ALL THE BAD PARTS OF YOUR TIME HERE
BUT IF YOU CAN HOLD AND KEEP THE LOVELIEST PARTS

IF  YOU  CAN  HOLD  THEM  -  KEEP  THEM  IN  YOUR  HEART

WITHOUT IT HURTING YOU
WITHOUT IT VEXING YOU TERRIBLY

THEN  HOLD  THEM  THERE

our times

H O W E V E R

IF IT BE TOO MUCH FOR YOU TO HOLD ME THERE
IN YOUR HEART
IN YOUR MIND
THEN PLEASE JUST LET ME GO

P L E A S E

IF THE MEMORIES OF OUR LOVE AND OUR BEAUTIFUL SUMMER
HURTS YOU ACHES YOU BREAKS YOU OR TRIPS YOU UP OR IN ANY WAY
HOLDS YOU BACK FROM BEING ALL THAT'S BEST IN YOU
IF IT KEEPS YOU FROM BEING HAPPY

THEN  LET  THEM  GO
i'd rather be forgotten than a cross you bear ...

I ' M  GOING  TO  HOLD  US  FOR  A  WHILE

UNTIL I IMAGINE THIS LETTER FINDS YOU
UNTIL I IMAGINE YOU GET TO READ IT
UNTIL I IMAGINE YOU GET TO TERMS WITH IT
UNTIL I IMAGINE YOU HAVE HOPED AGAINST HOPE AND TRIED TO HOLD US IN YOUR HEART AND MIND

AND  I  TOO  WILL  TRY  TO  KEEP  IT  AND  PROTECT  IT

AND THEN WHEN I'VE IMAGINED IT'S GETTING YOU STUCK AS IT HAS ME
I'M GOING TO LET MYSELF LET US GO
I'LL FORCE IT IF I HAVE TO

PLEASE  DON'T  BE  MAD  AT  ME
unless it helps you to let me go

Y O U  C A N  E V E N  H A T E  M E

HATE ME IF YOU WANT TO
HATE ME IF YOU NEED TO

i can't be the event that ruined your life ...

SO  AS  YOU  SEE  MORE  TEARS  ARE  HITTING  THE  PAGE
i'm sorry for all of it

BUT  EVEN  NOW  I  WOULD  DO  IT  ALL  AGAIN
for that love that feeling for you and i and us

OUR TIME
OUR SUMMER
OUR SECRET CAMP

OUR  BEAUTIFUL  FLEETING  LOVE
it was so fine i feared it - they say it's better to have loved and lost ...

BEAUTIFUL THINGS SUCH AS THAT DON'T EXIST IN MY WORLD
AND MAYBE NOT IN YOURS
AND IF THEY DO THEY MOST CERTAINLY CANNOT LAST

I HAVE NEVER LOVED ANYONE THIS WAY AND I NEVER WILL AGAIN

but i want you to be free

PLEASE LIVE
PLEASE LOVE
HAVE BABIES IF YOU WANT
HAVE IT ALL

let me go


Mo ghrá thú,



Loa

ps

I T   E N D E D   I N   S H E L T A

HOLD ME FOR A WHILE
AND WHEN YOU ARE READY
READ THIS ONE MORE TIME

T H E N   C O U N T   T O   T H R E E   A N D   B E   F R E E   O F   M E   F O R E V E R

I'LL DO IT WITH YOU

you were the love of my life

ain
do
trê

Another Envelope

NO RETURN ADDRESS                                              NO POSTAGE
NO NOTHING




                        INSIDE OF WHICH
                        T H E R E W A S




A    N    O    T    H    E    R        L    E    T    T    E    R

The Second Letter

T H E R E   W A S   N O

NO POSTAGE
NO ADDRESS
NO NOTHING

I T   W A S   F R E S H

DON'T KNOW WHAT THAT EVEN MEANS BUT IF YOU SAW IT AND FELT IT
THAT'S WHAT YOU'D SAY
IT WAS FRESH

I T   W A S   A   F R E S H   L E T T E R

    Hey handsome,

    I'm writing to tell you the truth
    Because you deserve to know
    Years ago Loa wrote to let you go
    Class act she was in that
    She said she was never pregnant to ease your mind
    She was
    She lied
    She had it taken care of and it was difficult, as there's no
    proper abortion back then - so we done it with plants and
    potions - the old ways - a poison of sorts, but it was painless
    It was yours - a boy
    Later, when pregnant with Joe's child, she done it again
    To hurt him, to spite him - but this time back-alley style to
    kill it, rip it apart - to hurt it - to hurt Joe and herself
    She nearly bled out

H E   S T O O D   I N   A   D A Z E

    Hey handsome,

    I'm writing to tell you the truth
    Because you deserve to know

A N D   H E   R E A D   I T   A G A I N

AND HE HURT
AND IT BROKE HIM IN A WAY
BROKE HIM ALL UP AGAIN

T H E   W O R D S   R I P P E D   H I M   F R O M   T H E   F L O W   O F   T I M E

time left him there and alone

G U T T E D

he stood and cried the paper stained by snot and tears he had wiped his face with it

a N d   h e   j U s T   k I N d a   c r U M p l e d

like the paper in his hand

HE   WISHED   HE   HAD   SOME   WHISKEY

but he didn't

SO HE JUST FELT IT
AND FELT IT AND FELT IT THERE FOR WHAT FELT LIKE FOREVER

he woke up on the floor where he had been reading

N U M B

the tears washed all the hate away

until he felt nothing

n o t h i n g

N O T H I N G

no thing

N O T H I N G   B U T   B R O K E N

*what the fuck is this life?*

*do not read it again do not read it again do not read it again do not read it again do not*

HE   FUCKING   READ   IT   ANYWAY

    Hey handsome,

    I'm writing to tell you the truth
    Because you deserve to know

*just stop reading it ...*

HE   COULDN'T

    Hey handsome,

    I'm writing to tell you the truth
    Because you deserve to know


HE   CAME   APART


T   H   E       W   O R D S     C A M E       AP A   R     T

it     a l l     ca m e       a p   a r t

E   V   ERY     T       H     I   N   G     ca m e     a p     a r t

c   A   M   E         A p a r t
i   n       t   w   o       p   a   r   t   s
into      little      pieces   in      two
a   n   d   t   w   o       p   a   r   t   de pa r ted
I   T         B   R   O   K   E         H   I   S
t   h   e       l   e   tt   e   r   s         c   a
the       let ters   of       t he       letters
h       e                         l   e   t                         h       e   r
he   le t   h   e   r         tears       he       t   e   a   r   s
t   h   e   y       b   r   o   k   e         a   pa r t
B   E   C   A   U   S   E       Y   O   U       D   E   S   E   R   V   E       T   O
S   H   E       W   A   S       S   H   E       W   A   S       W   A   S

B   E     C     A     U     S     E             s   h   e
  a s h       a n d       l i e s       a l s o         s h e
O     L     D             W     A     Y     S

s h   e       d i e   d       a   l s o       she       di   d

D   E   S   E   R   V   E       E               T   O
n   o       s   o   n       w   a   s       s   a   i   d
B.   E   C   A   U   S   E       O   F       Y   O   U       U       K   N   O   W
Y   O   U             D   E   S       e   R   V       E
she   nearly   bled   out   she   bled
Y O U       D E S E R V E       H E R       B L O O D       H E RE
        s       h       e           y   e   a   r   n   s
Y O U       D   E   S   E   R   V   E           I   T       S O N
Y O U R       S O N       B L E D       O U T       Y O U
k   n   o   w   n   o   w   u   k now   you   de serve   it
n       o       w           y   o   u               k   n   o   w

i      n      t      o              p      a      r      t      s

   t      h      e      y      c      a      m      e        a  p    ar      t

li   t    t    l    e          pi ec es      in      too   little peace

pa   r    ted      t    hey      a  re        a  p    ar    t      they a re

H    E    A    R    T              A    N    D          M    I    N    D

me      ap a  r t          a        p        a    r    t    i    n    g
letters          came          apart
come          apart      he      left        her

t      e      a      r      s          h    er        apart her        t e a r s

a    s          h      e          br o k e          a      p      a      rt

K    N  O  W    Y  O  U          D  E      S      E  R  VE      IT  Y O U        K  N  OW

S  H  E              S      A  W          S  H  E      S  A  W          A  S              W  A  S


l      i      e      d              Y      O      U                      k    n    o    w

died          you          deserve          as  h          and          l i e s

       P            O            I            S            O            N


d i d      s h e      d i e      s h e          d i e s          h e          d i e d


k      n      o      w          N      O      W          n    o    t    h    i    n    g

s      a      d          d    a    y              o    f        p    o    i    s    o    n

D    E    S    E    R    V    E          O    L    D          P    O    I    S    O    N          U.          KN  O  W

2      n    o      n    o        n    o        n    o      n    o        N  O

t o o      d e a r l y          h    o    w          r e d        h e r          b l o o d

U      B E          T  H  E          C  A  U  S  E          O  F          H  E  R          B L O O D

h      e      r              p    o    i    s    o    n              s    o    n

I  T      W  A  S      Y  O  U          p    o    i    s    o    n        b  o  y

R      P  O I S ON          Y  O  U              K  N  O  W          Y  O  U

u  r      d e v i o u s          y  ou  r        p      o i s o n    b l o o d

w    h    a    t              y    o    u              d    es        er    v    e hE  s  TaY ED   BRO kEN   TheR  E

uNTiL soMeHOw

T h E   L   Et TE R S   o F   Th E    LeT T E R S

STARTEDTAKING SHAPE AGAIN AND BROUGHT HIM BACK INTO TIME

HE STARED BLANK AS THE HOLLOW WITHIN HIM

HE SAW THERE WAS MORE AND READ IT

it said

now here's what we're going to do ...

www.ingramcontent.com/pod-product-compliance
Lightning Source LLC
Chambersburg PA
CBHW072221150726
48002CB00005B/1921